St. Cyril of Jerusalem's

Lectures on the

Christian Sacraments

1-78

£1-49.

⑦

K

D1628685

St. Cyril of Jerusalem's Lectures on the Christian Sacraments

THE PROCATECHESIS AND
THE FIVE MYSTAGOGICAL CATECHESES

EDITED BY

F. L. CROSS

Lady Margaret Professor of Divinity
in the University of Oxford
and Canon of Christ Church

ST VLADIMIR'S SEMINARY PRESS
Crestwood, New York 10707
1977

First published in 1951 by SPCK
This edition 1977
St Vladimir's Seminary Press
Crestwood, New York 10707

Printed in Great Britain

ISBN 0-913836-39-7

NOTE

THIS edition of St. Cyril's *Procatechesis* and five *Mystagogical Catecheses* has been prepared primarily to meet a pressing need in the Faculty of Theology at Oxford. But it is believed that others may welcome an opportunity of acquainting themselves, for the first time or afresh, with this group of lectures, which have an interest all their own and not least in their bearing on contemporary liturgical discussions. An introduction has been added.

The translation at the end of the volume is that prepared by R. W. Church for the *Library of the Fathers*. It has commended itself both for its many felicities of language and as possessing a historic interest as Church's first piece of published work. As Church used the Benedictine edition, his version occasionally presupposes a slightly variant Greek text from that in the present volume. But to have modified it for the sake of conformity would have sacrificed the integrity of what, despite occasional lapses of which he was himself aware in his later years, is perhaps a minor theological classic. The divergences will, it is hoped, be sufficiently patent to cause no embarrassment to the student.

F.L.C.

CHRIST CHURCH
OXFORD
20 April 1951

ACKNOWLEDGEMENT

Acknowledgement is due to the Dacre Press (A. & C. Black, Ltd.) for permission to quote from *The Shape of the Liturgy*, by Dom Gregory Dix.

TABLE OF CONTENTS

TABLE OF DATES

INTRODUCTION

§ i. *The Historical Background*

THE six lectures printed in the following pages were delivered at Jerusalem in the middle of the fourth century. They belong to a time of rapid transition and great significance in the history of the Church. Less than forty years before, Christianity was a proscribed faith; and the havoc wrought by the severest of the persecutions, traditionally associated with the name of Diocletian but more properly to be ascribed to his Caesar, Galerius, was still a living memory. In 306 Constantius Chlorus had died at York. In the next years his son and successor began his triumphant subjugation of the West. At some unrecorded place on a march on Rome which was to change the face of Europe, Constantine saw in the noonday sky (if Eusebius' account in the *Vita Constantini*, which professes to come from the Emperor himself, can be trusted) a luminous Cross superimposed on the sun with the legend 'By this conquer' (τουτῷ νίκα). The seal was set on its message when Maxentius was routed at the Milvian Bridge just outside the City on 28 October 312.

From then onwards Constantine showed marked partiality to the Christian cause. Early in 313 a policy of toleration was agreed upon between himself and Licinius, even if the 'Edict of Milan' in its traditional form be a myth. The new attitude to the Church is

reflected in Constantine's first dealings with the Donatists; and before long the new policy had its influence
on imperial legislative enactment. From 318 onwards
any civil suit might be transferred to the jurisdiction of
a Christian bishop if both parties agreed. In 321
bequests to the Church were legalized and the manu-
mission of slaves carried out in church before the bishop
was given full legal authority. In the East the emancipa-
tion of the Church was delayed a few years longer. In
the decade after the agreement in Italy the attitude of
Licinius to the Christians was undecided: and as the rift
between himself and Constantine grew wider he increasingly identified himself with the pagan cause. In
his last years he resorted, it would seem, to open perse-
cution of the Christians. But his power was short-lived.
After the decisive Battle of Chrysopolis, now finally
fixed at 18 September 324, Constantine was supreme in
East and West. Henceforward a pro-Christian policy
was adopted throughout the Empire, though the formal
establishment of the Christian Faith had to wait until
Theodosius the Great half a century later.

§ ii. *The Arian Controversy*

When Constantine reached the East in 324, he
found the Church troubled by a serious dispute. A rift
threatening to become ever wider had arisen on a matter
of fundamental doctrine (how fundamental on its theological side Constantine at first failed to realize, and to
the Church itself its gravity became fully manifest only
as the century proceeded) concerning the Person of the

Redeemer. Was Christ God? And if so, in what sense? The controversy which Arius had kindled had already spread over a large part of the East, and in an age when the Church, possessed of a well-established method of discipline for local disputes, was as yet ill practised in dealing with wider conflicts, appeal was made to the Emperor. The student wholly persuaded of the sincerity of Constantine's attachment to Christianity—and the scepticism of earlier scholars (J. Burckhardt, E. Schwartz) has gradually dissolved under the influence of a more thorough study of the documents by historians such as Professor N. H. Baynes, A. Alföldi, and A. H. M. Jones—need not deny that Constantine also saw in the new faith a useful and much-needed instrument for political cohesion. To reach a settlement he followed closely the course which he had already adopted in the West in connexion with the Donatists, and early in 325 convoked a Council of Bishops from as wide an area of the Empire as possible. It was planned to meet at Ancyra, but the place was changed to Nicaea, where it assembled in the early summer of 325.

The Nicene Council provided the Church with a doctrinal formula, and a permanent one, for the Homoousios has been virtually unchallenged among Christian theologians for nearly sixteen centuries. But though the term adopted proved to be that needed to express Christian belief in the status of the Redeemer, the Council did not immediately lead to theological unanimity. In the absence of a sufficiently large body of informed theologians to uphold the Nicene formula, the earlier tensions began to make themselves felt again shortly after the Council, and a reaction set in. Year by year the movement away from Nicaea gathered strength. Constantine died in 337; and when his son, Constantius II, the new emperor of the East, became an avowed supporter of the Arian cause, the sees in the East were increasingly filled with Arian bishops. In the next two decades Arian influences gained in strength, reaching their high-water mark in the concluding years of Constantius' reign.[1]

In the middle fifties philosophical theology took a fresh turn. A new movement arose which aimed at an interpretation of the central dogma of the Christian faith in terms acceptable to those trained in the philosophical schools. At first chary of the Nicene terminology it took Homoiousios rather than Homoousios as its watchword, but its whole tendency was in the orthodox direction. Its founder was Basil of Ancyra, and among its chief representatives were such men as Eustathius of Sebaste, Eleusius of Cyzicus, and George of Laodicea. The radical change in the political situation after Constantius' death on 3 November 361 added strength to the movement, for Julian's professed indifference to Christian theological niceties put an end to the repression of orthodoxy, and his successor, Jovian, was an avowed Nicene. By the time of Jovian's death (16 February 364) the current had set so strongly

---

[1] 'Ingemuit totus orbis, et Arianum se esse miratus est.' Jerome, *Dialog. adv. Lucif.* 19 (*P.L.* xxiii. 172 C); of the year 359.

in the direction of orthodoxy that the professed Arian sympathies of Jovian's successors in the purple might delay, but could not hinder, its restoration. In the seventies the Homoiousian movement was given a twist in the direction of stricter orthodoxy by the three Cappadocians, Basil of Caesarea, Gregory of Nazianzus, and Gregory of Nyssa, and the last political obstacles to the restoration of orthodoxy were removed when Valens was killed at Adrianople on 9 August 378. At a Council held at Constantinople in 381, and known to history as the 'Second Ecumenical Council', the Nicene formula was formally ratified.

§ iii. *Jerusalem*

During these years the importance of Jerusalem as a Christian metropolis was rapidly increasing. The part which, on a human reading, the Gospels might seem to have predestined for the city in Christian history for a long time appeared very unlikely to be realized. The Lord's disciples were soon scattered far and wide, while the small Christian community at Jerusalem was poverty-stricken and stood somewhat apart from the main stream of Church life. A generation had barely passed before the city ceased also to be the centre of Judaism. It was almost destroyed in A.D. 70, and after the rising under Barcochba in 132 finally razed to the ground. On the ruins Hadrian founded a wholly pagan city, 'Aelia Capitolina', in which the ancient sanctuary was covered by a forum and a capitol. Only very gradually did Jerusalem assume an important place in

Christian history and from then on as the home of a purely Gentile Christian community. In the third century we hear of Christian bishops. But far from their having any position of special privilege as occupants of the throne of the mother Church of Christendom, they were subject to the authority of the neighbouring see of Caesarea.

It was not until the fourth century that Jerusalem rose to a position of prominence. In 325 one of the Nicene canons determined that on the ground of 'custom and ancient tradition' its bishop should have the place of special honour, but without prejudice to the proper dignity of the metropolitical see of Caesarea.[1] Later in the century a struggle began in which Jerusalem strove to gain her ecclesiastical independence. Victory was achieved in the middle of the next century through the ruthless methods of Juvenal, Bishop of Jerusalem from 420 to 458. At the ·Council of Ephesus (431) he had maintained that even Antioch ought to be subject to the 'Apostolic see of Jerusalem', while at Chalcedon in 451 he at last secured for Jerusalem the coveted patriarchal rank.

The unique position which Jerusalem came to fill in the Christian consciousness arose from its association with the facts of the Lord's earthly life. The Holy Places soon won the interest of Constantine and his mother, Helena, who visited the city in 326. No less

---

[1] Ἐπειδὴ συνήθεια κεκράτηκε καὶ παράδοσις ἀρχαία, ὥστε τὸν ἐν Αἰλίᾳ ἐπίσκοπον τιμᾶσθαι, ἐχέτω τὴν ἀκολουθίαν τῆς τιμῆς, τῇ μητροπόλει σωζομένου τοῦ οἰκείου ἀξιώματος. Can. 7.

than four important sites were crowned with new
churches, built under Imperial supervision and at the
public expense—two in Jerusalem itself, the third on
the Mount of Olives, and the fourth at Bethlehem. Of
the two at Jerusalem the more important was a complex of buildings erected over the scene of the Lord's
Passion. From the full account in Eusebius[1] we deduce
that it consisted of three structures: the *Anastasis*, a
round building, erected over the site of the Holy
Sepulchre; the *Martyrium*, a much larger oblong
basilica on the spot where the Cross was found; and
the *Calvary*, a small structure open to the heavens on
the supposed site of the Crucifixion. These buildings
were put in hand shortly after the Imperial visit. In
335, to mark the Emperor's *Tricennalia*, a large Council
was summoned to Jerusalem and the church solemnly
dedicated.[2]

---

[1] *Vita Constantini*, 3. 23–30.

[2] Ibid. 4. 43. Our indebtedness to Eusebius, with his historical
and topographical interests added to the inspiration of local Palestinian patriotism, for giving to the earthly Jerusalem an ideological
significance has not always been sufficiently recognized. His Bibli-
cal writings, as well as such 'aids' as his 'Chronicle' and *Onoma-
sticon*, abundantly testify to his interest in O.T. and N.T. sites alike.
He must have known Jerusalem well; e.g. for the purposes of his
Ecclesiastical History he supplements the Library at Caesarea with
that of Bishop Alexander at Jerusalem (*H.E.* 6. 20). And from *c.* 313,
as Metropolitan of Caesarea, he had a personal, if ill-defined, responsi-
bility for the Holy City. It is difficult to see who but Eusebius, with
his close personal relationships with the Imperial family, could have
aroused the interest of Constantine and his mother in the Palestinian
sites. Nor can there be any reasonable doubt that he was the author of
can. 7 of Nicaea, with its defence of Hierosolymitan interests. The

§ iv. *Pilgrimages*

This new interest in the holy places, fostered by Imperial patronage, soon attracted innumerable pilgrims to Palestine. Christians from far and wide were filled with a longing to worship at the very sites where the Lord had lived. Nowhere else in Christendom were there such associations; and a visit to Palestine could alone bring the believer into historic contact with the events of the Gospel. Moreover, Palestine pos-

suggestion, apparently due to A. P. Stanley and accepted by J. B. Lightfoot and others, that the canon reflects a 'passage of arms' at the Council between Eusebius and his suffragan, Macarius, Bishop of Jerusalem, is wholly without support. The canon was designed rather as a counterweight to the privileges accorded to the cities named in can. 6 (Rome, Alexandria, Antioch), all of them filled in 325 by orthodox (and therefore to Eusebius objectionable) bishops and no doubt particularly against the last see, occupied by the extreme Homoousian, Eustathius. The concluding words of can. 7 were a natural safeguard of the position of Caesarea, and no more implied a 'passage of arms' than when a modern Anglican bishop on instituting a cleric to a benefice safeguards in the Deed of Institution his rights in his cathedral church. If there were any real conflict, something more forcible than a genitive absolute would have been needed. From 325 onwards Eusebius' active enthusiasm for the Holy Places is convincingly demonstrated by the *Vita Constantini* (passim). The Council of Jerusalem of 335, for Eusebius a second Nicaea (*V.C.* 4. 47), with the dedication of the magnificent new buildings erected under his inspiration, was as great a triumph for his topological enthusiasms as for his Arianizing theology. At the celebrations it was he, not Macarius, who extolled its glories in a sermon before the Emperor (ibid. 45), as in the following year it was he, the aged prelate, who was selected to go to Constantinople to deliver a discourse (which unhappily no longer survives) on the Holy Sepulchre. Without Eusebius devotion to the Holy Places might never have arisen.

sessed two further attractions. It contained the chief
sites associated with the Patriarchs and Prophets and
Kings of the Old Testament dispensation, sites in
which Constantine had also shown his interest. And it
was quite near to Egypt which, with its rapidly developing monastic communities, was soon to become an object
of hardly less interest to pious travellers than Palestine
itself as 'the second holy land' (L. Duchesne). A
stream of Roman ladies of noble family was drawn to
a life of devotion in Palestine, largely under the influence of St. Jerome. Melania the Elder, a young Roman
widow of Spanish blood, reached Palestine in 371 and
forthwith, with the material help of one of her sons,
founded the large convent for nuns where she was to
foster the religious life for over twenty-five years. In
August 385 Jerome and his younger brother, Paulinian,
set out from Rome for their long stay in the East,
arriving in Palestine in 386. Here they were joined by
Paula and her daughter, Eustochium, Paula being
specially commended by Jerome for her refusal to be
received by the proconsul before she had visited the
sacred places.[1] Their enthusiasm is reflected in the
glowing account which they sent from their newly
found paradise to their friend Marcella, urging her to
leave Rome and join them.[2] The whole movement was
given new and material encouragement by Theodosius
the Great, even if the account of his own pilgrimage to
Jerusalem given by Cedrenus[3] be without historical

---

[1] Jerome, *ep.* 108. 9. The whole letter is a long encomium of Paula.
[2] 'Jerome', *ep.* 46.   [3] *P.G.* cxxi. 617 A.

basis. The last decade of the fourth century witnessed what has now become the best known of all the pilgrimages. In the years 393–6[1] Etheria (formerly 'Silvia'), a rich lady whose concerns were more those of the modern tourist of pious leanings and ecclesiastical interests than the ideals of the ascetic Melania and Paula, reached Palestine after a long voyage from Spain. Her detailed record, with its account of the ceremonies of Palm Sunday and Holy Week, makes the *Peregrinatio*

---

[1] So G. Morin, 'Un passage énigmatique de saint Jérôme contre la pèlerine espagnole Eucheria', in *Revue Bénédictine*, xxx (1913), pp. 174–86. But recently in a most interesting paper, 'De datum der *Peregrinatio Egeriae* en het feest van Ons Heer Hemelvaart' (*Sacris Erudiri*, Jaarboek voor Godsdienstwetenschappen, i (1948), pp. 181–205), Dom E. Dekkers of Steenbrugge has argued with great acumen for 415–17. He follows A. Lambert, *Revue Mabillon*, 1936, pp. 71–94, 1937, pp. 1–24, and 1938, pp. 49–69 in identifying Egeria (*sic*) with the woman *huc illucque currentem* to whom Jerome refers in *ep*. 133. 4 (ad Ctesiphontem). Dekkers finds striking confirmation of this date (and this is the main thesis of his paper) in the fact that in 417 the fortieth day after Easter, i.e. 'Ascension Day', fell on 31 May, which according to a Georgian Kanonarion was the dedication date of the basilica at Bethlehem. Here, he thinks, lies the explanation of the passage in *Peregrinatio*, 42 f., which has long perplexed liturgists. It shows us why the 'station' should have been in that particular year at Bethlehem and not at the scene of the Ascension, the Imbomon on the Mount of Olives. Etheria could on that occasion appropriately write of the priests as preaching at Bethlehem *apte diei et LOCO*. The chief ground for hesitating to accept this conclusion is the late date of the Georgian calendar in question. As Dekkers admits, the commemoration is not found in the earlier Armenian calendar, published by F. C. Conybeare. It should be noted that the date 385, originally proposed by J. F. Gamurrini and still commonly accepted (e.g. G. Dix, *The Shape of the Liturgy*, pp. 348, 437) rested on the supposed identity of the authoress of the *Peregrinatio* with Silvia, the sister of the consul Rufinus.

Etheriae one of the most important liturgical documents of the fourth century.

§ v. *Liturgy*

One notable consequence of these pilgrimages was that Jerusalem became a liturgical influence second to none in Christendom. As A. Baumstark[1] has pointed out, the interest in the Lord's earthly life which contact with the sacred sites aroused gave a wholly new orientation to the liturgy. In earlier times Christian worship had been supra-historical in its relationship to the Lord's humanity. There was the one annual feast of Easter (the Passover), and this festival had commemorated simultaneously the Incarnation, the Redemption, the Resurrection, and the Ascension, that is, the whole range of God's redemptive activity for mankind. But the effect of the interest in the historic aspects of Christ's life was to bring about a differentiation. A whole cycle of separate feasts from Christmas to Ascension Day gradually came into being and led to the creation of the Christian Year. There thus arose what Abbot Fernand Cabrol, and after him Dom Gregory Dix, have called the Sanctification of Time. What is more, the enthusiastic accents in which returning pilgrims told of the splendours of Jerusalem led the Holy City to set the liturgical fashion in many distant places in Christendom. In at least three matters, all attested by Etheria, Jerusalem practice influenced the Roman rite, viz. (1) the Feast of the Presentation of Christ in the Temple;

[1] *Liturgie Comparée*, pp. 167 f.

(2) the Palm Sunday Procession; and (3) the Adoration of the Cross on Good Friday.[1]

§ vi. *Life of St. Cyril*

These few details of the historical, topographical, and liturgical setting of Cyril's life may help to supplement the meagre biographical details which have survived.[2] From his long connexion with Jerusalem it has generally been supposed that he was born there. He was ordained deacon by Macarius, Bishop of Jerusalem, *c.* 335, and priest by Maximus, Macarius' successor, *c.* 345. On Maximus' death[3] he succeeded to the bishopric (*c.* 350). With Jerusalem still subject to Caesarea Cyril must have owed his appointment to the Arianizing Acacius, Bishop of Caesarea, but this is no sufficient reason for accepting the statement in Jerome's *Chronicon* that Cyril obtained it by concessions to Arianism. In the following years tensions increased, partly, it may be, through dogmatic differences, but probably more from jealousy over the constantly growing importance of Cyril's see, and in 357 Cyril was deposed at a Council in Jerusalem. He took refuge in Tarsus, but he was restored by the Council at Seleucia in the next year

---

[1] A. Baumstark, op. cit., pp. 149–61.

[2] The chief early authorities are Epiphanius, *haer.* 73; Jerome, *vir. ill.* 112; Rufinus, *h.e.* 10. 24; Socrates, *h.e.* 2. 38 and 40; Sozomen, *h.e.* 4. 20 and 25; and Theodoret, *h.e.* 2. 22.

[3] The view of Socrates (2. 38), repeated *more suo* in Sozomen (4. 20), that Maximus was banished for his orthodoxy and Cyril intruded as an Arianizer is contradicted by Theodoret (2. 22) and by the Synodal Letter of the Council of Constantinople of 382 (*ap.* Thdt. *h.e.* 5. 9).

but one, only to be banished again by Acacius in 360. With the other exiled bishops he regained his see in 362 on Julian's accession and must have witnessed the Emperor's bizarre attempt to restore the Temple. The death of Acacius in 366 did not prevent yet another banishment under the Emperor Valens in 367. Not until Valens' death eleven years later (378) could he return. Of this long exile nothing is known. After his restoration he took an active part in reorganizing his Church. He was one of the 150 orthodox Fathers at the Second Ecumenical Council of Constantinople of 381, and in the synodal letter of the complementary council of the following year was referred to in terms of veneration. He died on 18 March 386, the day on which his feast is kept in both Eastern and Western Calendars. Apart from the *Catecheses*, his only surviving writings are some brief pieces of uncertain authenticity—a Sermon on the Pool of Bethesda, an Epistle to Constantius, and three short fragments.

§ vii. *The Catechetical Lectures*

The *Catechetical Lectures*, to which alone Cyril owes his fame, fall into two groups. All but the last five were addressed to the group of candidates[1] looking forward to Baptism at the coming Easter, who formed a special class known as φωτιζόμενοι (*competentes*); the last five

---

[1] The view commonly held until recently that there was a series of several stages in the catechumenate, corresponding with the stages of penance, has been seriously challenged by F. X. Funk, though E. Schwartz has shown that Funk's interpretation of the evidence needs some modification.

were directed to the newly baptized. It was the practice for the φωτιζόμενοι to give in their names on the eve of the first Sunday of Lent, and on the next day to make public profession of their purpose before witnesses. On the day following, the exorcisms and catecheses began, which continued daily through the Lent Fast. These catecheses took the form of continuous addresses, not catechizing by question and answer. Any of the faithful (baptized) who wished were permitted to be present, but catechumens of the earlier stage were excluded.

If for the moment the traditional view of their authorship be adopted, twenty-four of Cyril's *Catecheses* in all survive: an introductory 'Procatechesis', eighteen Catecheses addressed to the φωτιζόμενοι, and five further 'Mystagogical Catecheses' to the neophytes after their Baptism, delivered in the course of the Paschal Octave. Whereas the pre-baptismal *Catecheses* were given in constantine's great basilica on Golgotha already mentioned (cf. 16. 4), the *Mystagogical Catecheses* were preached at the Anastasis, i.e. at the small chapel which contained the Holy Sepulchre. If Cyril is correct in his statement that they were delivered fully seventy years after Probus, they date from A.D. 347 or perhaps a year or two later. This date has commonly been held to imply that Cyril delivered them while still a presbyter, though J. Mader[1] has argued that Cyril succeeded Maximus as Bishop early in 348 and that the lectures date from the Lent of that year. Their careful arrangement makes it highly improbable that they were delivered *ex*

---

[1] *Der heilige Cyrillus* (Einsiedeln, 1891).

tempore, though a note preserved in several of the manuscripts records that they were taken down in shorthand.

The first lecture in the *corpus*, the 'Procatechesis', which unlike the *Catecheses* proper was addressed to the catechumens in the presence of the whole congregation, is introductory. Cyril stresses the gravity of the step which the candidates are about to take and draws out the need for repentance and due preparation. He warns them that the very graces which Baptism brings will strengthen the determination of the powers of evil to ensnare them. The existence of the *disciplina arcani* in fourth-century Jerusalem is shown by his insistence that the φωτιζόμενοι are not to disclose what they will be taught, even to the ordinary catechumens.

Of the eighteen *Catecheses Illuminandorum*, the first five (1–5) deal with general topics while the remainder (6–18) are based on the successive articles of the Jerusalem Creed.[1] The latter group is of the first importance for the early history of the Creeds, for they enable us to reconstruct the text of the Creed which was extant at Jerusalem in Cyril's time. Moreover, as Cyril's comments occasionally indicate improvements of which he believed it capable, they point to certain changes which Cyril actually made himself in the text of the Jerusalem Creed after he had become Bishop. Since the time of F. J. A. Hort it has been widely held, especially by

---

[1] F. Cabrol (*Les Églises de Jérusalem*, pp. 155–9) argued that this latter group were all delivered in the sixth and seventh weeks of Lent, and that the *redditio symboli* took place on Palm Sunday.

English scholars, that the present form of our Nicene Creed (the 'Niceno-Constantinopolitan Creed') was none other than Cyril's own revision of the Jerusalem Creed which the Catechetical Lectures presupposed, drawn up by Cyril to substantiate his orthodoxy at the Council of Constantinople of 381.[1]

The five *Mystagogical Catecheses* (19–23), addressed to the neophytes in the full flush of their post-baptismal enthusiasm, treat of the Sacraments. The first three deal with Baptism, including the accompanying chrismation (which may or may not be identical with Confirmation), the fourth with Eucharistic doctrine, and the fifth with the Eucharistic liturgy. A phrase in the last of the earlier Catecheses (18. 33, καθ᾽ ἑκάστην ἡμέραν ἐν ταῖς ἑξῆς τῆς ἑβδομάδος ἡμέραις) seems to look forward to a sixth, and it would be more natural for every day of the Paschal week to have its lecture, but whether, as F. Probst held,[2] a catechesis has been lost or there were never more than five is a matter on which evidence is wanting. We learn that in Etheria's time an interpreter was always present to translate these post-paschal catecheses from Greek into Syriac; and this custom may well go back to Cyril's day.

§ viii. *St. Cyril's Liturgical Evidence*

Cyril's *Mystagogical Catecheses* are of unique interest for the light which they throw on fourth-century liturgi-

[1] The usual account is open to considerable objections, however. Some of these I hope to develop elsewhere. On the whole subject cf. J. N. D. Kelly, *Early Christian Creeds* (1950), ch. x.

[2] *Die Liturgie des vierten Jahrhunderts und deren Reform*, p. 82.

cal practice. From the first three it is possible to reconstruct a clear picture of the contemporary Baptismal
rite. After assembling in the vestibule of the baptistery
(ὁ προαύλιος τοῦ βαπτιστηρίου οἶκος; also ὁ ἐξώτερος οἶκος),
the candidates, facing west and with hands stretched
out, made a formal renunciation of the devil. Then,
turning to the east, they solemnly professed faith in
the Trinity and in the One Baptism of Repentance.
Passing into the inner chamber (ὁ ἐσώτερος οἶκος) they
next took off their clothes and were anointed with
exorcized oil. They were then led by the hand one by
one to the font ('the sacred pool of Holy Baptism',
20. 4), where after again making formal profession of
their faith they were immersed three times in the
blessed (cf. 3. 3) baptismal water to symbolize the
Redeemer's three-day sojourn in the grave. This was
followed by the post-Baptismal chrismation, and after
putting on white garments, the neophytes (νεοφώτιστοι,
lit. 'newly enlightened') made their way carrying
lighted tapers from the baptistery into the church
where they received their first Communion.

Of no less interest is Cyril's account of the Eucharist.
Indeed, the last of the *Mystagogical Catecheses* pre-
serves more details about the liturgy than any other
Eastern source of so ancient a date. We can already
see the Jerusalem Eucharistic rite assuming the more
definite shape which it reached in the Greek and Syriac
'Liturgies of St. James'.[1] Since the special purpose of
this catechesis was to make the newly baptized familiar

[1] For the connexions cf. G. Dix, *The Shape of the Liturgy*, pp. 187–96.

with the part of the service from which they had
hitherto been excluded, an account of the earlier half
of the rite is wanting. Cyril speaks only of what happens
after the dismissal of the catechumens (the *missa
fidelium*, as opposed to the *missa catechumenorum*) and
even here his witness is selective and incomplete.
Particular importance attaches to his mention of the
Epiclesis, since it is the earliest clear evidence for the
belief which identifies the conversion of the elements
with the petition to the Holy Ghost. Cyril thus stands
at the fountain-head of the tradition, characteristic of
Eastern theology, for which the Invocation of the
Spirit is the consecratory act, as contrasted with the
Western view that the change is brought about by
the recitation of the Words of Institution. Professor
E. C. Ratcliff[1] is doubtful whether Cyril's rite contained
an Institution narrative at all; its absence from the
primitive East Syrian liturgy of *Addai and Mari* shows
that it was not universal in early times. But Cyril's
description is fragmentary, and the existence of an
Institution Narrative is perhaps indicated by the cita-
tion at 22. 1. Another interesting liturgical point is the
occurrence of the *Paternoster* in this Eastern source, for
which other early evidence comes mainly from the

---

[1] In *The Study of Theology*, ed. K. E. Kirk (1939), p. 434. Cf. also
Professor Ratcliff's important paper, 'The Original Form of the
Anaphora of Addai and Mari; a Suggestion', in *J.T.S.* xxx (1928–9),
pp. 23–32. The Words of Institution are absent from all manuscripts
of *Addai and Mari*, though they were inserted in the (only) printed
text of the Liturgy, issued by the Archbishop of Canterbury's Mission
(Urmi, 1890). Cf. also G. Dix, *The Shape of the Liturgy*, p. 198.

West. It is absent from *Apostolic Constitutions* VIII and also (apparently) from the rite known to John Chrysostom.[1] But it is attested for Milan by St. Ambrose, *De Mysteriis* (c. 395) ; and St. Augustine[2] writing in Africa some twenty years later asserts that almost the whole world concludes the Eucharistic Prayer with it. Among further practices for which Cyril is the first witness may be mentioned the rinsing of the celebrant's hands before the Anaphora, the τὰ ἅγια τοῖς ἁγίοις, the *Sanctus* with the preceding Preface, and the Communion Anthem. He has no mention of the Anamnesis, but this, like the Words of Institution, was certainly in the Jerusalem rite by the middle of the fifth century.

Such is the tradition of the Jerusalem Church to which Cyril bears witness. If, as there is every reason to believe, Cyril was still a presbyter[3] when he delivered the *Catechetical Lectures*, he could as yet have had little influence himself on the liturgy. Only after he became bishop would he be in a position to adapt it to his own ideals. And though the personal influence which Cyril later exercised as bishop is largely a matter of inference, there can be little doubt, in view of the fact that Jerusalem was undergoing rapid development in liturgical

---

[1] It is found, of course, in the familiar 'Liturgy of St. John Chrysostom', now in current use in the Orthodox Church. Cf. F. E. Brightman, *Liturgies Eastern and Western* (1896), p. 339. But this liturgy has no claim to be connected with the Chrysostom of history.

[2] *Ep.* 149. 16, 'Fere omnis ecclesia dominica oratione concludit'.

[3] Even if J. Mader's view be accepted (cf. above, p. xxii), Cyril would still have been following traditional practice in the first few months of his episcopate.

practice during the years of his episcopate, that Cyril, with his practical instincts, fostered this growth. Indeed it is almost possible to see the creation of the liturgical year, already referred to, in Cyril's hands. For whereas the subjects of the *Catecheses*, though admittedly determined by the pattern of the Creed, make it quite clear that in 348 the Christian Year did not yet exist (since such a sermon as Catechesis 14 on the Resurrection, which has all the notes of an Easter sermon, would have been impossible in the latter part of Lent if it did), almost certainly[1] before Cyril's death the whole of Holy Week from Palm Sunday onwards was an established institution in Jerusalem. And who but Cyril could have brought about the change?

A penetrating estimate of Cyril's far-reaching influence on liturgical development is given by Dr. Dix:

'Cyril's Holy Week and Easter cycle is at the basis of the whole of the future Eastern and Western observances of this culminating point of the christian year. He gave to christendom the first outline of the public organisation of the divine office; and the first development of the proper of the seasons as well as of the saints. He was certainly the great propagator, if not the originator, of the later theory of eucharistic consecration by the invocation of the Holy Ghost, with its important effects in the subsequent liturgical divergence of East and West. In the

---

[1] This qualification is necessary, for the evidence comes from *Etheria* (393-6); but Etheria is reporting established practice. On the date cf. above, p. xviii.

Jerusalem church in his time we first find mention of liturgical vestments, of the carrying of lights and the use of incense at the gospel, and a number of other minor elements in liturgy and ceremonial, like the *lavabo* and the Lord's prayer after the eucharistic prayer, which have all passed into the tradition of catholic christendom. Above all, to him more than to any other single man is due the successful carrying through of that universal transposition of the liturgy from an eschatological to an historical interpretation of redemption, which is the outstanding mark left by the fourth century on the history of christian worship.'[1]

§ ix. *St. Cyril's Theology*

The wider aspects of Cyril's theology find no place in his *Mystagogical Catecheses* and hence do not call for detailed discussion here. We may safely conclude that in his earlier life he was at any rate no ardent Nicene, for Acacius would not have put a whole-hearted supporter of Athanasius into the see of Jerusalem; and Rufinus in the next generation implies some inconstancy in his relations with orthodoxy.[2] A close study of his writings has convinced a modern historian that in his *Catecheses*, 'Cyril tacitly protests against the ὁμοούσιον as of human contrivance (5. 12) and uses in preference the words "like to the Father according to the Scriptures" or "in all things" '.[3] Cyril also warns his hearers

[1] *The Shape of the Liturgy*, pp. 350 f.
[2] 'aliquando in fide, saepius in communione variabat' (*h.e.* 1. 23).
[3] A. Robertson, *Athanasius*, p. xlix.

against the special bugbears of the Arianizers, Sabellius
(11. 13) and Marcellus of Ancyra (15. 27). What this all
came to in terms of orthodoxy it is not easy to say.[1]
Probably Cyril's bent of mind was too practical to be
really interested in such questions. For R. Seeberg
Cyril was the typical Homoiousian.[2] On the other
hand, A. Harnack concluded that he was substantially
orthodox and that only the word ὁμοούσιος was wanting.[3] Some of his subordinationist expressions may be
due to his preferring the simple picture-language of
Scripture to the precise definitions of the speculative
theologian.

The main theological interest of the *Mystagogical
Catecheses* lies in the light which they throw on Cyril's
Sacramental beliefs. Baptism is essential to salvation,
the only alternative to water-baptism being the baptism
of blood in martyrdom (3. 4). Its effects are twofold,
forgiveness and sanctification. 'Baptism purges our sins
and conveys to us the gift of the Holy Spirit' (20. 6).
It is the 'holy indelible seal' (σφραγὶς ἁγία ἀκατάλυτος,
procat. 16). In procat. 16 Cyril epitomizes its effects as
'ransom for the captives, remission of offences, death
of sin and regeneration of the soul' (αἰχμαλώτοις λύτρον·

[1] The evidence is collected by J. Lebon, *R.H.E.* xx (1924), pp. 181–
210, 357–86.

[2] *Lehrbuch der Dogmengeschichte*, Bd. ii (ed. 2, 1910), pp. 94 f.

[3] *History of Dogma*, E.T., iv, p. 71 n. 3. Cf. the verdict of J. Lebon,
art. cit., p. 371: 'S'il n'en a pas la formule officielle (ὁμοούσιος τῷ
πατρί), saint Cyrille tient, dès l'époque des Catéchèses, toute la réalité
et toute la vérité du contenu doctrinal de la définition nicéenne'
(p. 371).

ἁμαρτημάτων ἄφεσις· θάνατος ἁμαρτίας· παλιγγενεσία ψυχῆς). Baptism is thus at once a grave and a mother (20. 4). In this connexion Cyril makes, however, an interesting contrast. While 'remission of sins is given equally to all', 'the communication of the Holy Ghost is bestowed according to each man's faith' (1. 5). In the matter of the rebaptism of heretics, he agrees with the earlier African practice. Heretics are to be 're-baptized', since their former washing was no real baptism (procat. 7).

How far the Chrismation described in the third *Mystagogic Catechesis* corresponds to what we call 'Confirmation' is disputed. Its occurrence almost immediately after the Baptismal immersion makes it difficult to say whether Cyril thought of it as a really distinct rite at all. By a natural symbolism it was associated with the anointing with the Spirit (21. 1), and Cyril asserts that this anointing makes us true Christs (χριστοί, cf. χρῖσμα) and invests us with the panoply of the Holy Ghost (τὴν πανοπλίαν τοῦ ἁγίου πνεύματος). The way in which he stresses this connexion of Chrismation with the gift of the Holy Ghost has led Cyril's authority to be invoked by such theologians as F. W. Puller,[1] A. J. Mason,[2] and A. C. A. Hall[3] (against, e.g., Darwell Stone[4]) in defence of the doctrine that this

[1] *What is the Distinctive Grace of Confirmation?* A Paper read before the Chapter of the South-eastern Division of the Upper Llandaff Rural Deanery (1880), pp. 28 f.

[2] *The Relation of Confirmation to Baptism* (ed. 2), pp. 336–48.

[3] *Confirmation* (1900), pp. 72 f.

[4] *Church Quarterly Review*, xlv (Jan. 1898), pp. 357–82, esp. 370.

Gift becomes the full possession of the Christian only at Confirmation, and that in Baptism the Spirit is conveyed in only a restricted sense. It may be questioned, however, whether St. Cyril's position in this issue can really be profitably discussed, since to do so is to apply to the undifferentiated Sacramental beliefs of early times categories which derive from the more elaborated theology of the medieval and post-medieval Church.

In his Eucharistic doctrine Cyril makes a definite advance on his predecessors. He is the first theologian to interpret the Lord's presence in conversionist language, forming a link between his predecessors and the more developed theology of St. Gregory of Nyssa. He illustrates what happens from the change of the water into wine at Cana (Jn. 2. 1–11), maintaining that the transformation is effected by the Holy Spirit since 'all that the Spirit touches is consecrated and changed' (ἡγίασται καὶ μεταβέβληται, 5. 7). In other passages he applies the words 'type' (τύπος) and 'antitype' (ἀντί-τυπον) to the material elements; and what he means by these words is indicated by passages where he speaks of Joshua as having been the type (τύπος) of Christ (10. 11), of Baptism as an antitype (ἀντίτυπον) of the sufferings of Christ (20. 6), and of Chrismation as 'the antitype of the Holy Ghost' (τοῦ ἁγίου πνεύματος τὸ ἀντίτυπον) (21. 1). When the Lord's body and blood enter into our members, we are mystically united with Christ in such a way that we become of one body and of one blood with Him (σύσσωμος καὶ σύναιμος αὐτοῦ, 22. 1), and may be reckoned as 'Christophers' (χριστοφόροι; 22. 9). An illustration of Cyril's realism is his sense of awe in the presence of the Eucharistic elements. He applies to the rite the epithets 'holy and most terrible' (ἁγία καὶ φρικωδεστάτη). In this matter he stands in marked contrast to the Cappadocian Fathers, though the conception is carried much farther in Chrysostom and the later Greek liturgies.[1]

Cyril's high theology of the Eucharist finds further expression in his sacrificial language. In this sacrifice we offer Christ who has been slain as a victim (Χριστὸν ἐσφαγισμένον). The sacrifice is propitiatory (θυσία τοῦ ἱλασμοῦ), for others as well as for ourselves (ὑπὲρ αὐτῶν τε καὶ ἡμῶν). Cyril's theology here bears relation to a developing conception of the Eucharist. Earlier theology had tended to think of the Eucharistic action as primarily the work of Christ; Cyril conceives it rather as the work of the whole Godhead, in which the part played by the Incarnate Christ is passive.[2]

§ x. St. Cyril's Place in History

Even when full allowance is made for the fact that the *Catecheses* were addressed, not to a theologically proficient audience, but to catechumens and newly baptized,[3] the impression we gain of Cyril is of a man of predominantly pastoral instincts, of good sense, conciliatory and essentially practical. He had little interest

[1] Fear and awe attaching to the Eucharistic Service', Appendix II to R. H. Connolly, O.S.B., 'The Liturgical Homilies of Narsai' in *Cambridge Texts and Studies*, viii. 1 (1909), pp. 92-7.

[2] Cf. G. Dix, *The Shape of the Liturgy*, pp. 278, 280.

[3] Cf. E. Bishop's note, *J.T.S.* xiv (1912-13), pp. 57-9.

in the doctrinal controversies which left such a deep
mark on his age, still less in speculation for its own sake.
We miss in him the theological penetration of the
Cappadocians or even the dogmatic concern of an
Athanasius. But he was eminently qualified by his
method of teaching, direct, straightforward, and to the
point, to give catechetical instruction. His tempera-
ment and outlook go far to explain the ever-growing
liturgical movement at Jerusalem. Indeed, at a time
when the attention of Christendom was being directed
afresh to the complex of events which form the
temporal basis of the Gospel, it was singularly
appropriate that a bishop such as Cyril, unmoved by
the partisan politics or theological speculations of his
day, should have presided over the fortunes of the
Church at the historic centre of the Christian world.

§ xi. *Manuscripts*

Apparently no systematic study of the textual evidence has ever been made. The more important manuscripts include:

1. Cod. Monacensis gr. 394 (saec. x). Formerly at
   Augsburg, whence with the rest of the Augsburg
   collection it passed to Munich in 1806.
2. Cod. Ottobonianus 86 (saec. x or xi). Vat. gr. 602
   (saec. xvi) is a copy of this MS.
3. Cod. Vindobonensis 55 (saec. incerti; collated by
   J. Müller, 1848, and used by J. Rupp).
4. Cod. Bodleianus Thos. Roe 25 (saec. xi).
5. Cod. Ottobonianus 446 (saec. xv).

6. Cod. Coislinianus 227 (ol. 101) in the Bibliothèque Nationale.

7. Cod. Monacensis gr. 278 (saec. xvi).

The text in the present volume does not pretend to be more than a revision of those already in print.

§ xii. *Editions*

The *Mystagogical Catecheses* were apparently edited for the first time, with a Latin version, by J. Grodecius (Vienna) in 1560. A second edition, with a selection of other *Catecheses*, followed by G. Morel (Paris) in 1564. The first complete edition of the whole work is due to J. Prévot (Paris, 1608). Far superior was that of Thomas Milles, Vice-Principal of St. Edmund Hall, Oxford, and later Bishop of Waterford (Oxford, 1703), and this in turn was further improved by the Benedictine, Dom A. A. Touttée (completed after his death in 1718 by P. Maran; Paris, 1720). This last is the text reprinted in J. P. Migne, *P.G.* xxxiii, cols. 331–1180. Later editions are due to the German scholars W. C. Reischl and J. Rupp (Munich, 1848–60) and, more recently (for the *Mystagogical Catecheses*), to H. Lietzmann (portions only; *Kleine Texte*, No. 5, 1903), G. Rauschen (1907), and J. Quasten (1936), the two latter in the *Florilegium Patristicum*. A rare edition of some interest (Procatechesis and 1–18 only) is that of Denys Cleophas and Photius Alexandrides (2 vols., Jerusalem, 1867–8).

The earliest printed English version of the *Catecheses*

appears to be that in the *Library of the Fathers* (1838).
The translation (reproduced in the present volume) was
the work of R. W. Church, the preface (interesting and
important as a statement of the Tractarian view of the
Fathers) by J. H. Newman. A revision of this translation was published by E. H. Gifford in the *Nicene and
Post-Nicene Christian Fathers* (1893) with a useful introduction and Greek index. Another English version will
be found in H. de Romestin's edition (1887).

§ xiii. *Authenticity*

As long ago as the first years of the seventeenth
century, doubts were cast on the genuineness of Cyril's
Catechetical Lectures, but less, it would seem, for critical
reasons than through Protestant objections to the high
Sacramental teaching, particularly of the *Mystagogical
Catecheses*. Until recent times these doubts were generally held to have been disposed of by T. Milles and
A. A. Touttée, especially by the latter's 'Dissertatio
secunda'.[1] In our own generation, however, scruples
about the *Mystagogical Catecheses* have again been expressed, first by T. Schermann[2] in a paper in the
Theologische Revue, x (1911), cols. 575–9, and at much
greater length by W. J. Swaans in a study in *Le
Muséon*, lv (1942), pp. 1–43.

[1] 'De Scriptis S. Cyrilli ac potissimum de Catechesibus', *P.G.* xxxiii.
123–69.
[2] I have been unable to obtain first-hand access to Schermann's
paper. There is a critique by S. Salaville, 'Une Question de Critique
Littéraire', *Échos d'Orient*, xvii (1915), pp. 531–7.

Schermann's objections (as reported by Salaville and Swaans) were based on the ground that the *Paternoster* in the liturgy implied a post-Cyrilline date. A measure of agreement with Schermann's doubts was expressed by Fr. J. A. Jungmann[1] on the similar ground that the attitude of 'awe' towards the Eucharistic species is not found elsewhere until a later time. Such considerations, however, are too uncertain to carry much weight. The liturgical data of the early Church are too scattered and sparse to permit of such deductions, and ideas as to their origin and provenance are open to constant revision with growing knowledge.

Dr. Swaans's more serious argument against the *Mystagogical Catecheses* rests on the evidence of the manuscripts. In Cod. Monac. gr. 394 the last five *Catecheses* are ascribed to John, Bishop of Jerusalem (386–417), i.e. Cyril's successor in the see; and this attribution finds some support from three other manuscripts, Ottobon. 86 and 466, and Monac. gr. 278—where the heading τοῦ αὐτοῦ Κυρίλλου καὶ Ἰωάννου ἐπισκόπου is held to be a conflation of the traditional with the real author. Dr. Swaans also maintains that the external attestation for the *Mystagogical Catecheses* is relatively late. The first writer who cites from *Catecheses* 19–23 as Cyrilline is the sixth- to seventh-century Eustratius, who is best known to history by his *Life* of Eutychius, Patriarch of Constantinople, who died in 582. In further

[1] J. A. Jungmann, S.J., *Die Stellung Christi im liturgischen Gebet*, Liturgiegeschichtliche Forschungen, Heft 7/8, Münster i. W., 1925, pp. 217 f.

support it has been claimed that there are certain stylistic differences between the first eighteen and the remaining five lectures.[1]

But against these considerations are to be set a number of cross-references between the two series of *Catecheses* which point to common authorship. The most emphatic is the passage in 18. 33 where Cyril explicitly refers to the further lectures which the candidates will hear in Easter Week after their baptism. And the contents of the *Mystagogical Catecheses* in fact correspond very closely with what Cyril there promises. It is true that there are five lectures, not six; but even if we are unwilling to grant that one has been lost, the fact that there was not a lecture *every* day (καθ' ἑκάστην ἡμέραν) can hardly be considered a serious objection. In 16. 26 and, rather less explicitly, in 13. 19 there are other statements which look forward to the post-Paschal lectures. And, on the other side, there are clear references in the *Mystagogical Catecheses* (19. 9, 23. 1) back to an earlier series.

These cross-references strongly support unity of authorship. It certainly cannot be said, despite a measure of approval given to their doubts by competent judges,[2] that the case against the *Mystagogical Cate-*

---

[1] So J. Quasten, *Monumenta Eucharistica et Liturgica Vetustissima*, Florilegii Patristici fasc. vii (Bonn, 1935), p. 70.

[2] Thus Marcel Richard expresses the view that Swaans 'paraît bien avoir définitivement résolu la question en faveur du successeur de Cyrille, Jean de Jérusalem', *Mélanges de Science Religieuse*, vi (1948), p. 282. J. de Ghellinck, S.J., *Patristique et Moyen Âge* (iii. 135 n.), also writes of their 'authenticité très compromise'. Cf. also E. Dekkers,

cheses has been proved. The manuscript evidence is the only real objection; and of this a ready explanation can be suggested. It must be remembered that the *Catecheses* were carefully prepared discourses and after delivery would almost certainly be preserved. With a fresh set of baptizands every year, there is every probability that, as is the way with modern Confirmation Addresses, they were repeated not once nor twice, but many times. If John succeeded Cyril in the office of Catechist as he later followed him in the episcopate, is it impossible that he too catechized his candidates with the same series of splendid addresses?

§ xiv. *Bibliography*

I. GENERAL BACKGROUND

Besides the standard Church Histories of L. Tillemont (still unsurpassed after nearly two and a half centuries), L. Duchesne, B. J. Kidd, and A. Fliche et V. Martin, valuable surveys are to be found in the *Cambridge Ancient History*, vol. xii (1939) and the *Cambridge Medieval History*, vol. i (1913). There are also many important and useful dictionary articles, notably in the *D.C.B.*, *D.T.C.*, *D.A.C.L.*, and *P.-W.*

On Constantine's relation with the Church:

J. Burckhardt, *Die Zeit Constantins des Grossen* (Basel, 1853).

E. Schwartz, *Kaiser Constantin und die christliche Kirche* (Leipzig, 1913).

N. H. Baynes, *Constantine the Great and the Christian Church.* The Raleigh Lecture on History for 1929 (London, 1930).

art. cit., p. 202 n. One hesitates to withhold assent when confronted with such an array of authority (and particularly M. Richard, who has an uncanny sense for the right answer in such matters), but to me at least the case still seems unproved.

A. Alföldi, *The Conversion of Constantine and Pagan Rome*. Eng. trans. by H. Mattingly (Oxford, 1948).

A. H. M. Jones, *Constantine and the Conversion of Europe* (London, 1948).

2. FOR THE LITURGICAL AND TOPOGRAPHICAL BACKGROUND

J. H. Srawley, *The Early History of the Liturgy* (The Cambridge Handbooks of Liturgical Study, ed. 2, Cambridge, 1947).

F. Probst, *Die Liturgie des vierten Jahrhunderts und deren Reform* (Münster i. W., 1893).

G. Dix, O.S.B., *The Shape of the Liturgy* (London, 1945), esp. pp. 187–203, 349–54.

A. Baumstark, *Liturgie Comparée*. Conférences faites au Prieuré d'Amay (Chevetogne, 1940).

F. Cabrol, 'Étude sur la Peregrinatio Silviae', *Les Églises de Jérusalem, la Discipline et la Liturgie au IVe Siècle* (Paris, 1895).

H. Vincent–F. M. Abel, *Jérusalem*. Recherches de Topographie d'Archéologie et d'Histoire, 2 vols. (Paris, 1914–26).

F. Cabrol, 'La Semaine Sainte et les Origines de l'Année Liturgique' in *Les Origines Liturgiques* (Paris, 1906).

J. B. Thibaut, *Ordre des Offices de la Semaine Sainte à Jérusalem* (Paris, 1926).

H. Leclercq, 'Pèlerinages', s.v. *Dict. d'Arch. chrét. et de Liturgie*.

Éthérie. Journal de Voyage. Ed. H. Pétré (Sources Chrétiennes, xxi, Paris, 1948).

3. CYRIL'S LIFE

E. H. Gifford, *Cyril of Jerusalem* (1893). Though somewhat antiquated, the Introduction contains the fullest account in English of Cyril and his writings.

G. Delacroix, *Saint Cyrille de Jérusalem. Sa Vie et ses Œuvres* (Paris, 1865).

J. Mader, *Der heilige Cyrillus, Bischof von Jerusalem, in seinem Leben und seinen Schriften* (Einsiedeln, 1891).

X. Le Bachelet, 'Cyrille de Jérusalem (saint)' in *Dictionnaire de Théologie Catholique*, iii (1908), cols. 2527–77.

4. CYRIL'S DOCTRINAL POSITION

G. Marquardt, *S. Cyrilli Hierosol. de Contentionibus et Placitis Arianorum Sententia* (Braunsberg, 1881).

J. Gummerus, *Die Homöusianische Partei bis zum Tode des Konstantius* (Leipzig, 1900).

J. Lebon, 'La Position de saint Cyrille de Jérusalem dans les Luttes provoquées par l'Arianisme', in *Rev. d'Hist. Eccl.* xx (1924), pp. 181–210, 357–86.

5. CYRIL AND THE CATECHUMENATE

J. Mayer, *Geschichte des Katechumenats und der Katechese in den ersten sechs Jahrhunderten* (Kempten, 1868).

L. L. Rochat, *Le Catéchuménat au quatrième Siècle d'après les Catéchèses de S. Cyrille à Jérusalem* (Geneva, 1875).

A. T. Kluck, 'Der Katechumenat nach dem hl. Cyrill von Jerusalem', in *Der Katholik*, Mainz, ii (1878), pp. 132 ff.

F. X. Funk, *Kirchengeschichtliche Abhandlungen und Untersuchungen*, Band i (Paderborn, 1897), esp. papers vi, vii, and viii.

E. Schwartz, *Bussstufen und Katechumenatsklassen* (Schriften der Wissenschaftlichen Gesellschaft in Strassburg, Heft 7) (1911).

A. Bludau, 'Der Katechumenat in Jerusalem im 4. Jahrhundert', in *Theologie und Glaube*, vi (1924), 225–42.

6. CYRIL AND THE JERUSALEM CREED

F. J. A. Hort, *Two Dissertations* (Cambridge, 1876).

7. THE AUTHENTICITY OF THE MYSTAGOGICAL CATECHESES

W. J. Swaans, 'A propos des "Catéchèses Mystagogiques" attribuées à S. Cyrille de Jérusalem', in *Le Muséon*, lv (1942), pp. 1–43.

THE PROCATECHESIS

1. *The Blessings to be expected from Baptism*

Ἤδη μακαριότητος ὀσμὴ πρὸς ὑμᾶς, ὦ φωτιζόμενοι, ἤδη τὰ νοητὰ ἄνθη συλλέγετε πρὸς πλοκὴν ἐπουρανίων στεφάνων· ἤδη τοῦ πνεύματος τοῦ ἁγίου ἔπνευσεν ἡ εὐωδία. Ἤδη περὶ τὸ προαύλιον τῶν βασιλείων γεγόνατε· γένοιτο δὲ καὶ ὑπὸ τοῦ βασιλέως εἰσαχθῆτε. Ἄνθη γὰρ νῦν ἐφάνη τῶν δένδρων· γένοιτο δὲ ἵνα καὶ ὁ καρπὸς τέλειος ᾖ. Ὀνοματογραφία τέως ὑμῖν γέγονε, καὶ στρατείας κλῆσις· καὶ νυμφαγωγίας λαμπάδες, καὶ οὐρανίου πολιτείας ἐπιθυμία, καὶ πρόθεσις ἀγαθή, καὶ ἐλπὶς ἐπακολουθοῦσα· ἀψευδὴς γὰρ ὁ εἰπών, ὅτι τοῖς ἀγαπῶσι τὸν θεὸν πάντα συνεργεῖ εἰς τὸ ἀγαθόν. Ὁ μὲν γὰρ θεὸς δαψιλής ἐστιν εἰς εὐεργεσίαν· περιμένει δὲ ἑκάστου τὴν γνησίαν προαίρεσιν. Διὰ τοῦτο ἐπήγαγεν ὁ ἀπόστολος λέγων, τοῖς κατὰ πρόθεσιν κλητοῖς οὖσιν· ἡ πρόθεσις γνησία οὖσα, κλητόν σε ποιεῖ· κἂν γὰρ τὸ σῶμα ὧδε ἔχῃς, τὴν δὲ διάνοιαν μὴ ἔχῃς, οὐδὲν ὠφελῇ.

2. *A Warning from Simon Magus*

Προσῆλθέ ποτε καὶ Σίμων τῷ λουτρῷ ὁ μάγος· ἐβαπτίσθη, ἀλλ' οὐκ ἐφωτίσθη· καὶ τὸ μὲν σῶμα ἔβαψεν ὕδατι, τὴν δὲ καρδίαν οὐκ ἐφώτισε πνεύματι· καὶ κατέβη μὲν τὸ σῶμα, καὶ ἀνέβη· ἡ δὲ ψυχὴ οὐ συνετάφη Χριστῷ, οὐδὲ συνηγέρθη. Ἐγὼ δὲ λέγω τὰς ὑπογραφὰς τῶν πτωμάτων, ἵνα μὴ σὺ ἐμπέσῃς. Ταῦτα γὰρ τυπικῶς ἐγένετο ἐκείνοις, γέγραπται δὲ πρὸς νουθεσίαν τῶν μέχρις σήμερον προσερχομένων. Μήτις ὑμῶν εὑρεθῇ πειράζων τὴν χάριν· μήτις ῥίζα πικρίας ἄνω φύουσα ἐνοχλῇ· μήτις ὑμῶν εἰσέλθῃ λέγων· Ἄφες ἴδωμεν τί ποιοῦσιν οἱ πιστοί· εἰσελθὼν ἴδω, ἵνα μάθω

τὰ γινόμενα. Ἰδεῖν προσδοκᾷς, τὸ δὲ ὀφθῆναι οὐ προσδοκᾷς;
καὶ νομίζεις, ὅτι σὺ μὲν πολυπραγμονεῖς τὰ γινόμενα, θεὸς
δὲ σοῦ οὐ πολυπραγμονεῖ τὴν καρδίαν;

3. The True Baptismal Garments

Ἐπολυπραγμόνησέ τίς ποτε τὸν γάμον ἐν τοῖς εὐαγγε-
λίοις· καὶ ἀνάξιον ἔνδυμα λαβὼν εἰσῆλθε, καὶ ἀνέπεσε, καὶ
ἔφαγε· συνεχώρησε γὰρ ὁ νυμφίος. Ἔδει δὲ αὐτὸν ἰδόντα
τὸ λευχειμονοῦν πάντων, καὶ αὐτὸν ἀναλαβέσθαι τοιοῦτον
ἔνδυμα. Ἀλλ᾽ ἴσων μὲν μετελάμβανε βρωμάτων· ἀνισότητα
δὲ εἶχε σχημάτων καὶ προαιρέσεως. Ἀλλ᾽ ὁ νυμφίος, εἰ καὶ
δαψιλής, ἀλλ᾽ οὐκ ἄκριτος· περιερχόμενος δὲ τῶν ἀνακει-
μένων ἕκαστον καὶ θεωρῶν, ἰδών τινα ἀλλότριον, μὴ ἔχοντα
γάμου ἔνδυμα, ἔλεγε πρὸς αὐτόν· Ἑταῖρε, πῶς εἰσῆλθες
ὧδε; ποίῳ χρώματι; ποίᾳ συνειδήσει; ἔστω, ὁ θυρωρὸς οὐκ
ἐκώλυσε, διὰ τὸ δαψιλὲς τοῦ παρέχοντος· ἔστω, ἄγνοιαν
εἶχες ποταπῷ δεῖ σχήματι εἰσελθεῖν εἰς τὸ συμπόσιον·
εἰσῆλθες, εἶδες ἀστράπτοντα ὥσπερ τὰ σχήματα τῶν
ἀνακειμένων· οὐκ ἔδει σε κἂν ἐκ τῶν φαινομένων διδαχθῆναι;
οὐκ ἔδει σε ἐξελθεῖν εὐκαίρως, ἵνα καὶ εὐκαίρως εἰσέλθῃς;
Νῦν δὲ ἀκαίρως εἰσῆλθες, ἵνα ἀκαίρως ἐκβληθῇς. Καὶ
προστάσσει τοῖς ὑπηρέταις· Δήσατε αὐτοῦ πόδας, τοὺς
τολμηρῶς εἰσβάλλοντας· δήσατε αὐτοῦ χεῖρας, τὰς μὴ
εἰδυίας ἔνδυμα περιβαλέσθαι φαιδρόν· καὶ ἐκβάλετε αὐτὸν
εἰς τὸ σκότος τὸ ἐξώτερον· ἀνάξιος γάρ ἐστι λαμπάδων
νυμφικῶν. Ἰδὲ τί συνέβη τῷ τότε· ἀσφάλισαι τὰ σεαυτοῦ.

4. The Need for due Preparation

Ἡμεῖς μὲν γάρ, οἱ διάκονοι Χριστοῦ, δεδέγμεθα ἕκαστον,
καὶ θυρωρῶν ὥσπερ τάξιν ἐπέχοντες, ἀνέτην ἀφήκαμεν τὴν

θύραν. Ἐγχωρεῖ δέ σε βεβορβορωμένην ἔχοντα τὴν ψυχὴν ἁμαρτίαις, καὶ τὴν προαίρεσιν ἐσπιλωμένην, εἰσελθεῖν. Εἰσῆλθες· κατηξιώθης· ὄνομά σου ἐνεγράφη. Βλέπεις μοι τὸ σεμνὸν τοῦτο τῆς ἐκκλησίας κατάστημα; θεωρεῖς μοι τάξιν καὶ ἐπιστήμην; γραφῶν ἀνάγνωσιν, κανονικῶν παρουσίαν, διδασκαλίας ἀκολουθίαν; δυσωπήθητι καὶ τὸν τόπον, καὶ παιδεύθητι ἐκ τῶν φαινομένων· ἔξελθε εὐκαίρως τὰ νῦν, καὶ εἴσελθε αὔριον εὐκαιρότατα. Εἰ φιλάργυρον ἔχεις τὸ σχῆμα τῆς ψυχῆς, ἄλλο ἐνδυσάμενος εἴσελθε· ἔκδυσαί μοι πορνείαν καὶ ἀκαθαρσίαν, καὶ ἔνδυσαί μοι σωφροσύνης λαμπροτάτην στολήν. Ἐγὼ παραγγέλλω, πρὶν ὁ νυμφίος τῶν ψυχῶν εἰσέλθῃ Ἰησοῦς, καὶ ἴδῃ τὰ σχήματα. Πολλή σοι ἡ προθεσμία· τεσσαράκοντα ἡμερῶν μετάνοιαν ἔχεις· ἔχεις πολλὴν εὐκαιρίαν καὶ ἐκδύσασθαι καὶ ἀποπλύνασθαι, καὶ ἐνδύσασθαι καὶ εἰσελθεῖν. Εἰ δὲ ἐπιμένεις κακῇ προαιρέσει, ὁ μὲν λέγων ἀναίτιος, σὺ δὲ μὴ προσδόκα λήψεσθαι τὴν χάριν· τὸ μὲν γὰρ ὕδωρ σε δέξεται, τὸ δὲ πνεῦμά σε οὐ δέξεται. Εἴ τις σύνοιδεν ἑαυτῷ τὸ τραῦμα, τὴν ἔμπλαστρον λαβέτω· εἴ τις ἔπεσεν, ἐγειρέσθω· μηδεὶς ἐν ὑμῖν Σίμων, μηδεμία ὑπόκρισις, μηδὲ περιεργία τοῦ πράγματος.

5. The Net of the Church

Ἐγχωρεῖ σε καὶ προφάσει ἄλλῃ ἐλθεῖν· ἐγχωρεῖ γὰρ καὶ ἄνδρα βούλεσθαι γυναικὶ καθικετεῦσαι, καὶ διὰ τοῦτο προσελθεῖν· ἀντιστρέφει καὶ ἐπὶ γυναικῶν τὸ ὅμοιον ὁ λόγος· καὶ δοῦλος πολλάκις δεσπότῃ, καὶ φίλος φίλῳ ἀρέσαι ἠθέλησε. Δέχομαι τὸ δέλεαρ τοῦ ἀγκίστρου, καὶ καταδέχομαί σε, κακῇ προαιρέσει μὲν ἐλθόντα, ἐλπίδι δὲ ἀγαθῇ σωθησόμενον. Ἴσως οὐκ ᾔδεις ποῦ ἔρχῃ, οὐδὲ ποία σε σαγήνη λαμβάνει· γέγονας εἴσω δικτύων ἐκκλησιαστικῶν· ζωγρήθητι· μὴ

φύγῃς· ἀγκιστρεύει γάρ σε Ἰησοῦς, οὐχ ἵνα θανατώσῃ, ἀλλ'
ἵνα θανατώσας ζωοποιήσῃ· δεῖ γάρ σε ἀποθανεῖν καὶ ἀνα-
στῆναι· ἤκουσας γὰρ τοῦ ἀποστόλου λέγοντος· Νεκροὶ μὲν
τῇ ἁμαρτίᾳ, ζῶντες δὲ τῇ δικαιοσύνῃ· ἀπόθανε τοῖς
ἁμαρτήμασι, καὶ ζῆσον τῇ δικαιοσύνῃ· ἀπὸ τοῦ σήμερον ζῆσον.

6. The Rewards of Vocation

Βλέπε μοι πηλίκην σοι ἀξίαν ὁ Ἰησοῦς χαρίζεται. Κατηχούμενος ἐλέγου, ἔξωθεν περιηχούμενος· ἀκούων ἐλπίδα,
καὶ μὴ εἰδώς· ἀκούων μυστήρια, καὶ μὴ νοῶν· ἀκούων
γραφάς, καὶ μὴ εἰδὼς τὸ βάθος. Οὐκ ἔτι περιηχῇ, ἀλλ'
ἐνηχῇ· τὸ γὰρ ἔνοικον πνεῦμα λοιπὸν οἴκους θείους τὴν
διάνοιάν σου ἐργάζεται. Ὅταν ἀκούσῃς τὰ περὶ τῶν
μυστηρίων γεγραμμένα, τότε νοήσεις ἃ μὴ ᾔδεις. Καὶ μὴ
νομίσῃς ὅτι μικρὸν πρᾶγμα λαμβάνεις· ἄνθρωπος ὢν οἰκτρός,
θεοῦ λαμβάνεις προσηγορίαν. Ἄκουε Παύλου λέγοντος·
Πιστὸς ὁ θεός· ἄκουε ἄλλης γραφῆς λεγούσης· Θεὸς
πιστὸς καὶ δίκαιος. Τοῦτο προβλέπων ὁ Ψαλμῳδὸς
ἔλεγεν ἐκ προσώπου τοῦ θεοῦ, ἐπειδὴ μέλλουσιν ἄνθρωποι
θεοῦ προσηγορίαν λαμβάνειν· Ἐγὼ εἶπα, θεοί ἐστε,
καὶ υἱοὶ ὑψίστου πάντες· ἀλλὰ βλέπε, μὴ πιστοῦ μὲν
ἡ προσηγορία, ἀπίστου δὲ ἡ προαίρεσις. Εἰσῆλθες εἰς
ἀγῶνα, κάμε τὸν δρόμον· ἄλλον καιρὸν τοιοῦτον οὐκ ἔχεις.
Εἴ σοι γάμων ἡμέραι προέκειντο, οὐχ ἂν κατεφρόνησας
πάντων, καὶ περὶ τὴν ἑτοιμασίαν τῆς ἑστιάσεως ἐγένου;
μέλλων δὲ τὴν ψυχὴν καθοσιοῦν τῷ ἐπουρανίῳ νυμφίῳ, οὐκ
ἀργήσεις σωματικῶν, ἵνα ἄρῃς πνευματικά;

7. Baptism may not be repeated

Οὐκ ἔνι δὶς καὶ τρὶς λαβεῖν τὸ λουτρόν· ἐπεὶ ἦν εἰπεῖν·

Ἅπαξ ἀποτυχών, δεύτερον κατορθῶ· ἐὰν δὲ τὸ ἅπαξ ἀπο-
τύχῃς, ἀδιόρθωτον τὸ πρᾶγμα. Εἷς γὰρ κύριος, καὶ
μία πίστις, καὶ ἓν βάπτισμα· μόνον γὰρ αἱρετικοί
τινες ἀναβαπτίζονται, ἐπειδὴ τὸ πρότερον οὐκ ἦν βάπτισμα.

8. The Need for a Right Purpose

Οὐδὲν γὰρ ἄλλο παρ' ἡμῶν ζητεῖ ὁ θεός, εἰ μὴ προαίρεσιν
ἀγαθήν· μὴ λέγε· Πῶς μου ἐξαλείφονται αἱ ἁμαρτίαι; Ἐγώ
σοι λέγω, τῷ θέλειν, τῷ πιστεύειν· τί τούτου συντομώτερον;
Ἐὰν δὲ τὰ μὲν χείλη σου λέγῃ τὸ θέλειν, ἡ δὲ καρδία μὴ
λέγῃ, καρδιογνώστης ὁ κρίνων. Ἄργησον ἀπὸ τῆς σήμερον
ἀπὸ παντὸς φαύλου πράγματος· μή σου λαλησάτω ἡ γλῶσσα
ἄσεμνα ῥήματα· μή σου τὸ βλέμμα ἁμαρτανέτω, μηδὲ
ῥεμβέσθω τὰ μὴ χρήσιμα.

9. In what spirit the Exorcisms are to be received

Οἱ δὲ πόδες σου εἰς τὰς κατηχήσεις σπευδέτωσαν. Τοὺς
ἐπορκισμοὺς δέχου μετὰ σπουδῆς· κἂν ἐμφυσηθῇς, κἂν
ἐπορκισθῇς, σωτηρία σοι τὸ πρᾶγμα. Νόμισον εἶναι ἀργὸν
χρυσόν, καὶ δεδολωμένον, ποικίλαις ὕλαις ἀναμεμιγμένον,
χαλκῷ, καὶ κασσιτέρῳ, καὶ σιδήρῳ, καὶ μολύβδῳ· ζητοῦμεν
τὸν χρυσὸν μόνον ἔχειν· χρυσὸς μὴ δύναται ἄνευ πυρὸς
καθαρθῆναι τὰ ἀνοίκεια· οὕτως ἄνευ ἐπορκισμῶν οὐ δύναται
καθαρθῆναι ψυχή· εἰσὶ δὲ θεῖοι, ἐκ θείων γραφῶν συνειλε-
γμένοι· ἐσκέπασταί σου τὸ πρόσωπον, ἵνα σχολάσῃ λοιπὸν
ἡ διάνοια· ἵνα μὴ τὸ βλέμμα ῥεμβόμενον ποιήσῃ ῥέμβεσθαι
καὶ τὴν καρδίαν. Τῶν δὲ ὀφθαλμῶν ἐσκεπασμένων, οὐκ
ἐμποδίζεται τὰ ὦτα δέξασθαι τὸ σωτήριον. Ὃν γὰρ τρόπον
οἱ τῆς χρυσοχοϊκῆς ἐργασίας ἔμπειροι, διά τινων λεπτῶν
ὀργάνων τὸ πνεῦμα τῷ πυρὶ παρεμβάλλοντες, καὶ τὸ ἐν τῇ

χώνῃ κεκρυμμένον χρυσίον ἀναφυσῶντες, τὴν παρακειμένην
ἐρεθίζοντες φλόγα εὑρίσκουσι τὸ ζητούμενον· οὕτω τῶν
ἐπορκιζόντων, διὰ πνεύματος θείου ἐμβαλλόντων τὸν φόβον,
καὶ ὥσπερ ἐν χώνῃ, τῷ σώματι. τὴν ψυχὴν ἀναζωπυρούντων·
φεύγει μὲν ὁ ἐχθρὸς δαίμων, παραμένει δὲ ἡ σωτηρία, καὶ
παραμένει ἡ ἐλπὶς τῆς αἰωνίου ζωῆς, καὶ λοιπὸν ἡ ψυχὴ
καθαρθεῖσα τῶν ἁμαρτημάτων ἔχει τὴν σωτηρίαν. Παρα-
μένωμεν τοίνυν τῇ ἐλπίδι, ἀδελφοί, καὶ δῶμεν ἑαυτούς, καὶ
ἐλπίσωμεν· ἵνα ὁ θεὸς τῶν ὅλων, τὴν ἡμετέραν προαίρεσιν
ἰδών, καθάρῃ μὲν ἡμᾶς τῶν ἁμαρτιῶν, ἐλπίδας δὲ ἡμῖν
ἀγαθὰς παράσχῃ τῶν πραγμάτων, καὶ δώῃ ἡμῖν μετάνοιαν
σωτηρίας. Θεὸς ἐκάλεσε, σὺ δὲ ἐκλήθης.

10. Catechizing and the Spiritual Conflict

Παράμενε ταῖς κατηχήσεσιν· εἰ καὶ πολλὰ παρατείνωμεν
λέγοντες, μήποτε ἡ διάνοιά σου ἐκλυθῇ· ὅπλα γὰρ λαμβάνεις
κατ' ἀντικειμένης ἐνεργείας· ὅπλα λαμβάνεις καθ' αἱρέσεων,
κατ' Ἰουδαίων, καὶ Σαμαρειτῶν, καὶ Ἐθνῶν· πολλοὺς
ἐχθροὺς ἔχεις, πολλὰ βέλη λάμβανε· πρὸς πολλοὺς γὰρ
ἀκοντίζεις· καὶ χρεία σοι μαθεῖν πῶς κατακοντίσῃς τὸν
Ἕλληνα, πῶς ἀγωνίσῃ πρὸς αἱρετικόν, πρὸς Ἰουδαῖον
καὶ Σαμαρείτην· καὶ τὰ μὲν ὅπλα ἕτοιμα, καὶ τὸ ξίφος τοῦ
πνεύματος ἑτοιμότατον· δεῖ δὲ καὶ δεξιὰς τείνειν διὰ
προαιρέσεως ἀγαθῆς, ἵνα πόλεμον κυρίου πολεμήσῃς, ἵνα
νικήσῃς ἀντικειμένας ἐνεργείας, ἵνα ἀήττητος γένῃ παντὶ
αἱρετικῷ πράγματι.

11. Edification through Catechesis

Παραγγελία δέ σοι καὶ τοῦτο ἔστω· τὰ λεγόμενα μάνθανε,
καὶ τήρει εἰς τὸν αἰῶνα. Μὴ νομίσῃς τὰς συνήθεις εἶναι

προσομιλίας· κἀκεῖναι μὲν γὰρ ἀγαθαί, καὶ πίστεως ἀξίαι·
ἀλλ᾽ ἐὰν σήμερον ἀμελήσωμεν, αὔριον μανθάνομεν· τὰ δὲ
περὶ τοῦ λουτροῦ τῆς παλιγγενεσίας κατ᾽ ἀκολουθίαν δια-
διδόμενα διδάγματα ἐὰν σήμερον ἀμεληθῇ, πότε κατορθω-
θήσεται; Νόμισόν μοι φυτείας εἶναι δένδρων καιρόν· ἐὰν
μὴ σκάψωμεν καὶ βαθύνωμεν, πότε δύναται ἄλλοτε καλῶς
φυτευθῆναι τὸ ἅπαξ κακῶς φυτευθέν; Νόμισόν μοι οἰκοδομὴν εἶναι τὴν κατήχησιν· ἐὰν μὴ βαθύνωμεν, καὶ θεμέλιον
θῶμεν, ἐὰν μὴ κατ᾽ ἀκολουθίαν δεσμοῖς οἰκοδομῆς ἁρμο-
λογήσωμεν τὸν δόμον, ἵνα μὴ εὑρεθῇ τι χαῦνον, καὶ σαθρὰ
γένηται ἡ οἰκοδομή, οὐδὲν ὄφελος οὐδὲ τοῦ προτέρου κόπου·
ἀλλὰ δεῖ κατ᾽ ἀκολουθίαν λίθον μὲν λίθῳ ἀκολουθεῖν, καὶ
γωνίαν γωνίᾳ ἕπεσθαι· ἀποξεόντων δὲ ἡμῶν τὰ περιττά,
οὕτως τελείαν οἰκοδομὴν ἀναβαίνειν· οὕτω προσφέρομέν σοι
λίθους ὥσπερ γνώσεως· δεῖ ἀκούειν τὰ περὶ θεοῦ ζῶντος·
δεῖ ἀκούειν τὰ περὶ κρίσεως· δεῖ ἀκούειν τὰ περὶ Χριστοῦ·
δεῖ ἀκούειν τὰ περὶ ἀναστάσεως· καὶ πολλά ἐστιν ἀκολούθως
λεγόμενα, νῦν μὲν σποράδην εἰρημένα, τότε δὲ καθ᾽ ἁρμονίαν
προσφερόμενα· ἐὰν δὲ μὴ συνάψῃς ἐν τῷ ἑνί, καὶ μνημονεύσῃς
τῶν πρώτων καὶ τῶν δευτέρων, ὁ μὲν οἰκοδομῶν οἰκοδομεῖ,
αὖ δὲ σαθρὰν ἕξεις τὴν οἰκοδομήν.

12. *The* Disciplina Arcani

Ὅτε τοίνυν ἡ κατήχησις λέγηται, ἐάν σε κατηχούμενος
ἐξετάσῃ, τί εἰρήκασιν οἱ διδάσκοντες, μηδὲν λέγε τῷ ἔξω·
μυστήριον γάρ σοι παραδίδομεν, καὶ ἐλπίδα μέλλοντος
αἰῶνος· τήρησον τὸ μυστήριον τῷ μισθαποδότῃ. Μή ποτέ
σοί τις εἴπῃ· τί βλάπτῃ, ἐὰν κἀγὼ μάθω; Καὶ οἱ νοσοῦντες
τὸν οἶνον ζητοῦσιν· ἀλλ᾽ ἐὰν ἀκαίρως δοθῇ, φρενῖτιν
ἐργάζεται· καὶ δύο κακὰ γίνεται, καὶ ὁ νοσῶν ἀπόλλυται, καὶ

ὁ ἰατρὸς διαβάλλεται· οὕτως ὁ κατηχούμενος, ἐὰν ἀκούσῃ
παρὰ πιστοῦ· καὶ ὁ κατηχούμενος φρενιτιᾷ, οὐκ οἶδε γὰρ
τί ἤκουσε, καὶ ἐλέγχει τὸ πρᾶγμα, καὶ ἐκμυκτηρίζει τὸ
λεγόμενον· καὶ ὁ πιστὸς ὡς προδότης κατακρίνεται. Ἤδη
δὲ σὺ ἐν μεθορίῳ στήκεις, βλέπε μοι μὴ ἐκλαλήσῃς· οὐχ ὅτι
οὐκ ἄξια λαλιᾶς τὰ λεγόμενα, ἀλλ' ὅτι ἡ ἀκοὴ ἀναξία τοῦ
δέξασθαι· ἧς καὶ σύ ποτε κατηχούμενος, οὐ διηγησάμην σοι τὰ
προκείμενα· ὅταν τῇ πείρᾳ λάβῃς τὸ ὕψωμα τῶν διδασκο-
μένων, τότε ἂν γνώσῃ, ὅτι ἀνάξιοι οἱ κατηχούμενοι τῆς ἀκοῆς.

13. *Proper Behaviour before Exorcism*

Μιᾶς μητρὸς γεγόνατε υἱοὶ καὶ θυγατέρες, οἱ ἀπογρα-
φέντες· ὅταν εἰσέλθητε πρὸ τῆς ὥρας τῶν ἐπορκισμῶν, εἰς
ἕκαστος ὑμῶν λαλείτω τὰ πρὸς εὐσέβειαν· κἄν τις ὑμῶν μὴ
παρῇ, ἐπιζητήσατε. Εἰς τράπεζαν εἰ ἐκλήθης, οὐκ ἂν περι-
έμενες τὸν συγκεκλημένον· ἀδελφὸν εἰ εἶχες, οὐκ ἂν τῷ ἀδελφῷ
τὸ ἀγαθὸν ἐζήτεις; Μὴ πολυπραγμόνει λοιπὸν πραγμάτων
ἀνωφέλειαν· μή, τί ἐποίησε πόλις; μή, τί ἐποίησε κώμη; μή,
τί ἐποίησε βασιλεύς; μή, τί ἐποίησεν ἐπίσκοπος; μή, τί
ἐποίησε πρεσβύτερος; Ἄνω βλέπε· ὁ καιρὸς ὁ σὸς ἐκείνου
χρείαν ἔχει. Σχολάσατε καὶ γνῶτε. ὅτι ἐγώ εἰμι ὁ
θεός. Ἐὰν ἴδῃς τοὺς πιστοὺς διακονοῦντας, καὶ μὴ μερι-
μνῶντας· ἔχουσι τὸ ἀσφαλές, οἴδασι τί ἔλαβον, κατέχουσι τὴν
χάριν· σὺ δὲ ἀκμὴν ἐν ζυγῷ στήκεις, ἢ δεχθῆναι, ἢ μὴ δεχθῆναι·
μὴ μιμήσῃ τοὺς ἔχοντας τὸ ἀμέριμνον, ἀλλὰ μέτελθε τὸν φόβον.

14. *The same subject, continued*

Καὶ ὅταν ἐπορκισμὸς γένηται, ἕως ὅτου οἱ ἄλλοι ἐπορκι-
ζόμενοι παραγένωνται, ἄνδρες μετ' ἀνδρῶν, καὶ γυναῖκες μετὰ
γυναικῶν. Νῦν γάρ μοι χρεία τῆς τοῦ Νῶε κιβωτοῦ· ἵνα ᾖ

Νῶε χωρὶς καὶ οἱ υἱοὶ αὐτοῦ· καὶ ἡ γυνή, καὶ αἱ γυναῖκες τῶν υἱῶν αὐτοῦ. Εἰ γὰρ καὶ μία ἦν ἡ κιβωτός, καὶ κεκλεισμένη ἦν ἡ θύρα· ἀλλὰ ἐσχημάτιστο τὰ πράγματα. Εἰ καὶ κέκλεισται ἡ ἐκκλησία, καὶ πάντες ὑμεῖς ἔνδον· ἀλλὰ διεστάλθω τὰ πράγματα, ἄνδρες μετ᾽ ἀνδρῶν, καὶ γυναῖκες μετὰ γυναικῶν· μὴ γένηται ἡ ὑπόθεσις τῆς σωτηρίας, πρόφασις ἀπωλείας· κἂν ἡ ὑπόθεσις καλή, πλησίον ἀλλήλων καθέζεσθαι, ἀλλὰ μακρὰν ἔστω τὰ πάθη. Εἶτα οἱ ἄνδρες καθεζόμενοι καὶ ἐχέτωσαν βιβλίον χρήσιμον· καὶ ὁ μέν τις ἀναγινωσκέτω, ὁ δέ τις ἀκουέτω· κἂν μὴ βιβλίον παρῇ, ὁ μὲν προσευχέσθω, ὁ δέ τι χρήσιμον λαλείτω. Καὶ ὁ ύλλογος πάλιν ὁ παρθενικὸς οὕτω συνειλέχθω, ἢ ψάλλων ἢ ἀναγινώσκων ἡσυχῇ· ὥστε λαλεῖν μὲν τὰ χείλη, μὴ ἀκούειν δὲ τὰ ἀλλότρια ὦτα. Γυναικὶ γὰρ λαλεῖν ἐν ἐκκλησίᾳ οὐκ ἐπιτρέπω· καὶ ἡ ἔγγαμος δὲ ὁμοίως μιμείσθω· καὶ προσευχέσθω, καὶ τὰ χείλη κινείσθω, φωνὴ δὲ μὴ ἀκουέσθω· ἵνα παρέλθῃ Σαμουήλ, ἵνα σου ἡ στεῖρα ψυχὴ γεννήσῃ τὴν σωτηρίαν θεοῦ ἐπακούσαντος. Ὁ γὰρ Σαμουὴλ ταύτην ἔχει τὴν ἑρμηνείαν.

15. *The true Paschal Enlightenment*

Ὄψομαι τὴν σπουδὴν ἑκάστου, ὄψομαι τὸ εὐλαβὲς ἑκάστης. Πυρούσθω ἡ διάνοια πρὸς εὐλάβειαν, χαλκευέσθω ἡ ψυχή, σφυροκοπείσθω τὸ σκληρὸν τῆς ἀπιστίας, ἀποπεσάτωσαν αἱ περιτταὶ τοῦ σιδήρου λεπίδες, μενέτω τὸ καθαρόν· ἀποπεσάτω τοῦ σιδήρου ὁ ἰός, μενέτω δὲ τὸ γνήσιον. Ποτὲ ὑμῖν δείξῃ ὁ θεὸς ἐκείνην τὴν νύκτα, τὸ σκότος τὸ ἡμεροφανές, περὶ οὗ εἴρηται· Σκότος οὐ σκοτισθήσεται ἀπὸ σοῦ, καὶ νὺξ ὡς ἡ ἡμέρα φωτισθήσεται· τότε ὑμῶν ἑκάστῳ καὶ ἑκάστῃ παραδείσου θύρα ἀνοιχθῇ. Τότε ὑδάτων ἀπολαύσητε Χριστοφόρων, ἐχόντων εὐωδίαν. Τότε Χριστοῦ

προσηγορίαν λάβητε, καὶ ἐνέργειαν θείων πραγμάτων. Ἤδη μοι
τῆς διανοίας τὸ ὄμμα ἀναβλέψατε· ἤδη μοι χοροὺς ἀγγελικοὺς
ἐννοήσατε, καὶ δεσπότην τῶν ὅλων θεὸν καθεζόμενον, υἱὸν
δὲ μονογενῆ ἐν δεξιᾷ συγκαθήμενον, καὶ πνεῦμα συμπαρόν,
θρόνους δὲ καὶ κυριότητας λειτουργοῦντας· καὶ ὑμῶν δὲ
ἕκαστον καὶ ἑκάστην, σωζόμενον καὶ σωζομένην. Ἤδη
ὑμῶν τὰ ὦτα ὥσπερ κατηχεῖσθαι ποιήσατε ἐκείνην τὴν
καλὴν ἠχήν, ὅτε ὑμῶν σωθέντων οἱ ἄγγελοι ἐπιφωνήσουσι·
Μακάριοι ὧν ἀφέθησαν αἱ ἀνομίαι, ὅτε, ὥσπερ
ἀστέρες τῆς ἐκκλησίας, εἰσέλθητε φαιδροὶ τῷ σώματι, καὶ
φωτεινοὶ τῇ ψυχῇ.

16. The Praise and true Meaning of Baptism

Μέγα, τὸ προκείμενον βάπτισμα· αἰχμαλώτοις λύτρον·
ἁμαρτημάτων ἄφεσις· θάνατος ἁμαρτίας· παλιγγενεσία ψυχῆς·
ἔνδυμα φωτεινόν· σφραγὶς ἁγία ἀκατάλυτος· ὄχημα πρὸς
οὐρανόν· παραδείσου τρυφή· βασιλείας πρόξενον· υἱοθεσίας
χάρισμα. Ἀλλὰ δράκων παρὰ τὴν ὁδὸν τηρεῖ τοὺς περι-
πατοῦντας. Βλέπε μὴ δάκῃ τῇ ἀπιστίᾳ. Βλέπει τοσούτους
σωζομένους, καὶ ζητεῖ τίνα καταπίῃ· Πρὸς πατέρα
πνευμάτων εἰσέρχῃ, ἀλλὰ δι᾽ ἐκείνου τοῦ δράκοντος διέρχῃ·
πῶς οὖν αὐτὸν διέλθῃς; Ὑπόδησαι τοὺς πόδας ἐν ἑτοι-
μασίᾳ τοῦ εὐαγγελίου τῆς εἰρήνης· ἵνα κἂν δάκῃ, μὴ
βλάπτῃ· πίστιν ἔνοικον ἔχε, κραταιὰν ἐλπίδα, κρηπῖδα
ἰσχυράν, ἵνα διέλθῃς τὸν ἐχθρόν, καὶ εἰσέλθῃς πρὸς τὸν
δεσπότην. Τὴν σαυτοῦ καρδίαν ἑτοίμασον εἰς ὑποδοχὴν
διδασκαλίας, εἰς κοινωνίαν ἁγίων μυστηρίων. Εὔχου πυκνό-
τερον, ἵνα ὁ θεός σε καταξιώσῃ τῶν ἐπουρανίων καὶ ἀθανάτων
μυστηρίων. Μήτε ἡμέραν ἄργει, μήτε νύκτα· ἀλλ᾽ ὅταν ὁ
ὕπνος ἐκ τῶν ὀμμάτων σου ἐκπέσῃ, τότε ἡ διάνοιά σου εἰς

προσευχὴν σχολαζέτω. Κἂν ἴδῃς λογισμὸν αἰσχρὸν ἀναβάντα εἰς τὴν διάνοιάν σου, λάβε κρίσεως ὑπομνηστικὸν σωτηρίας· σχόλασον τὴν διάνοιαν εἰς τὸ μαθεῖν, ἵνα ἐπιλάθῃ φαύλων πραγμάτων. Ἐὰν ἴδῃς τινά σοι λέγοντα· Καὶ εἰσέρχῃ εἰς τὸ ὕδωρ καταβῆναι; ἄρτι γὰρ οὐκ ἔχει ἡ πόλις βαλανεῖα; Γίνωσκε ὅτι ὁ δράκων τῆς θαλάσσης ταῦτά σοι κατασκευάζει· μὴ πρόσεχε τοῖς χείλεσι τοῦ λαλοῦντος, ἀλλὰ τῷ ἐνεργοῦντι θεῷ. Φύλασσε τὴν σαυτοῦ ψυχήν, ὅπως ἄληπτος γένῃ· ἵνα παραμείνας τῇ ἐλπίδι, κληρονόμος γένῃ σωτηρίας αἰωνίου.

17. The Responsibilities of our Vocation

Ἡμεῖς μὲν ταῦτα, ὡς ἄνθρωποι, καὶ παραγγέλλομεν καὶ διδάσκομεν. Μὴ ποιήσητε δὲ τὴν οἰκοδομὴν ἡμῶν χόρτον, καὶ καλάμην, καὶ ἄχυρα· ἵνα μὴ τοῦ ἔργου κατακαέντος, ζημιωθῶμεν· ἀλλὰ ποιήσατε τὸ ἔργον χρυσίον, καὶ ἀργύριον, καὶ λίθους τιμίους. Ἐν ἐμοὶ μὲν γάρ ἐστι τὸ εἰπεῖν, ἐν σοὶ δὲ τὸ προθέσθαι, ἐν θεῷ δὲ τὸ τελειῶσαι. Νευρώσωμεν τὴν διάνοιαν· συντείνωμεν τὴν ψυχήν· ἑτοιμάσωμεν τὴν καρδίαν· περὶ ψυχῆς τρέχομεν· περὶ αἰωνίων πραγμάτων ἐλπίζομεν. Δυνατὸς δὲ ὁ θεός, ὁ τὰς καρδίας ὑμῶν εἰδὼς καὶ γινώσκων τίς μέν ἐστι γνήσιος τίς δὲ ὑποκριτής, τὸν μὲν γνήσιον φυλάξαι, τὸν δὲ ὑποκριτὴν πιστοποιῆσαι. Δύναται γὰρ ὁ θεὸς καὶ τὸν ἄπιστον πιστοποιῆσαι, ἐὰν μόνον δῷ τὴν καρδίαν. Καὶ ἐξαλεῖψαι τὸ καθ᾽ ὑμῶν χειρόγραφον· ἀμνηστίαν δὲ ὑμῖν παράσχοι τῶν πρώτων παραπτωμάτων· φυτεύσοι δὲ ὑμᾶς εἰς τὴν ἐκκλησίαν, καὶ στρατεύσοι ὑμᾶς ἑαυτῷ, ὅπλα περιβαλὼν τῆς δικαιοσύνης· οὐρανίων δὲ πραγμάτων καινῆς διαθήκης πληρώσειε, καὶ πνεύματος ἁγίου σφραγῖδα δώῃ ἀνεξάλειπτον εἰς τοὺς αἰῶνας, ἐν Χριστῷ Ἰησοῦ τῷ κυρίῳ ἡμῶν, ᾧ ἡ δόξα εἰς τοὺς αἰῶνας τῶν αἰώνων. Ἀμήν.

MYSTAGOGICAL CATECHESES

Lecture I

THE PRE-BAPTISMAL RITES

Καὶ ἀνάγνωσις ἐκ τῆς Πέτρου καθολικῆς πρώτης ἐπιστολῆς ἀπὸ τοῦ νήψατε γρηγορήσατε, ἕως τέλους τῆς ἐπιστολῆς.

1. *The Purpose of these Lectures*

Ἐπόθουν ὑμῖν καὶ πάλαι, ὦ γνήσια καὶ περιπόθητα τῆς ἐκκλησίας τέκνα, περὶ τῶν πνευματικῶν τούτων καὶ ἐπουρανίων διαλεχθῆναι μυστηρίων. ἀλλ' ἐπειδὴ σαφῶς ἠπιστάμην, ὄψιν ἀκοῆς πολλῷ πιστοτέραν εἶναι, ἀνέμενον τὸν παρόντα καιρόν, ἵνα εὐπροσαγωγοτέρους ὑμᾶς περὶ τῶν λεγομένων ἐκ ταύτης λαβὼν τῆς πείρας εἰς τὸν φωτεινότερον καὶ εὐωδέστερον λειμῶνα τοῦδε τοῦ παραδείσου χειραγωγήσω· ἄλλως τε καὶ χωρητικοὶ τῶν θειοτέρων κατέστητε μυστηρίων, θείου καὶ ζωοποιοῦ βαπτίσματος ἀξιωθέντες. ἐπεὶ τοίνυν λοιπὸν τῶν ἐντελεστέρων δεῖ μαθημάτων παρατιθέναι τράπεζαν, φέρε ταῦτα ὑμᾶς ἀκριβῶς παιδεύσωμεν, ἵνα εἰδῆτε τὴν ἔμφασιν τὴν πρὸς ὑμᾶς κατ' ἐκείνην γεγενημένην τοῦ βαπτίσματος τὴν ἑσπέραν.

2. *The Need to renounce Satan*

Εἰσήειτε πρῶτον εἰς τὸν προαύλιον τοῦ βαπτίσματος οἶκον, καὶ πρὸς τὰς δυσμὰς ἑστῶτες ἠκούσατε, καὶ προσετάττεσθε ἐκτείνειν τὴν χεῖρα, καὶ ὡς παρόντι ἀπετάττεσθε τῷ σατανᾷ. χρὴ δὲ τοῦτο ὑμᾶς εἰδέναι, ὅτι ἐν παλαιᾷ ἱστορίᾳ οὗτος κεῖται ὁ τύπος. ὅτε γὰρ Φαραώ, ὁ πικρότατος καὶ ὠμότατος τύραννος, κατέθλιβε τῶν Ἑβραίων τὸν ἐλεύθερον λαὸν καὶ εὐγενῆ, ὁ θεὸς ἀπέστειλε τὸν Μωσῆν ἐξάγειν αὐτοὺς ἐκ τῆς πονηρᾶς τῶν Αἰγυπτίων δουλείας. καὶ αἵματι μὲν ἀμνοῦ ἐχρίοντο αἱ φλιαί, ἵνα φύγῃ ὁ ὀλοθρεύων τοὺς τὸ σημεῖον ἔχοντας τοῦ αἵματος οἴκους, παραδόξως δὲ ἠλευθεροῦτο ὁ τῶν Ἑβραίων λαός. ἐπειδὴ δὲ καὶ ἐλευθερωθέντας ὁ ἐχθρὸς κατεδίωξε καὶ παραδόξως εἶδε τὴν θάλασσαν αὐτοῖς τεμνομένην, ὅμως ἐχώρει, ἴχνη ἴχνεσι συμβάλλων, καὶ παραχρῆμα ὑποβρύχιος ἐγένετο καταποντούμενος ἐν θαλάσσῃ ἐρυθρᾷ.

3. *The New Redemption contrasted with the Old*

Μετάβηθί μοι λοιπὸν ἀπὸ τῶν παλαιῶν ἐπὶ τὰ νέα, ἀπὸ τοῦ τύπου ἐπὶ τὴν ἀλήθειαν. ἐκεῖ Μωσῆς εἰς Αἴγυπτον ἀπὸ τοῦ θεοῦ πεμπόμενος, ἐνταῦθα Χριστὸς ἐκ τοῦ πατρὸς εἰς τὸν κόσμον ἀποστελλόμενος· ἐκεῖ, ἵνα ἐξαγάγῃ λαὸν ἐξ Αἰγύπτου θλιβόμενον, ὧδε Χριστός, ἵνα ῥύσηται τοὺς ἐν τῷ κόσμῳ ὑπὸ τῆς ἁμαρτίας καταπονουμένους· ἐκεῖ αἷμα ἀμνοῦ ὀλοθρευτοῦ ἦν ἀποτρόπαιον, ἐνταῦθα τοῦ ἀμνοῦ τοῦ ἀμώμου Ἰησοῦ Χριστοῦ τὸ αἷμα δαιμόνων καθέστηκε φυγαδευτήριον. ἐκεῖνος ὁ τύραννος κατεδίωκεν ἕως θαλάσσης τὸν παλαιὸν ἐκεῖνον λαόν, καὶ σοὶ ὁ ἰταμός, ὁ ἀναίσχυντος καὶ ἀρχέκακος οὗτος δαίμων ἕως αὐτῶν ἠκολούθει τῶν σωτηρίων ναμάτων. ἐκεῖνος ὑποβρύχιος γέγονεν ἐν θαλάσσῃ, καὶ οὗτος ἐν τῷ σωτηρίῳ ὕδατι ἀφανίζεται.

4. *The Renunciation (1) of Satan*

Ἀλλ' ὅμως ἀκούεις τεταμένῃ τῇ χειρὶ ὡς πρὸς παρόντα εἰπεῖν· " ἀποτάσσομαί σοι, σατανᾶ." βούλομαι καί, τίνος νεκεν ἵστασθε πρὸς δυσμάς, εἰπεῖν· ἀναγκαῖον γάρ. ἐπειδὴ τοῦ φαινομένου σκότους τόπος αἱ δυσμαί, ἐκεῖνος δὲ σκότος τυγχάνων ἐν σκότῳ ἔχει καὶ τὸ κράτος τούτου χάριν

συμβολικῶς πρὸς δυσμὰς ἀποβλέποντες ἀποτάσσεσθε τῷ σκο-
τεινῷ ἐκείνῳ καὶ ζοφερῷ ἄρχοντι.

Τί οὖν ὑμῶν ἕκαστος ἑστὼς ἔλεγεν; ἀποτάσσομαί σοι,
σατανᾶ, σοὶ τῷ πονηρῷ καὶ ὠμοτάτῳ τυράννῳ, οὐκέτι σου
δέδοικα, λέγων, τὴν ἰσχύν. κατέλυσε γὰρ ταύτην Χριστὸς
αἵματός μοι καὶ σαρκὸς κοινωνήσας, ἵνα διὰ τούτων κατ-
αργήσῃ θανάτῳ τὸν θάνατον, ὅπως μὴ διὰ παντὸς ἔνοχος
γένωμαι δουλείας. ἀποτάσσομαί σοι τῷ δολερῷ καὶ πανουργο-
τάτῳ ὄφει. ἀποτάσσομαί σοι ἐπιβούλῳ ὄντι καὶ προσποιήσει
φιλίας πράξαντι πᾶσαν παρανομίαν καὶ ἐμποιήσαντι τοῖς
ἡμετέροις προγόνοις ἀποστασίαν. ἀποτάσσομαί σοι, σατανᾶ,
τῷ πάσης κακίας δημιουργῷ καὶ συνεργῷ.

5. And (2) of Satan's Works

Εἶτα ἐν δευτέρᾳ λέξει μανθάνεις λέγειν· "καὶ πᾶσι τοῖς
ἔργοις σου." ἔργα δὲ τοῦ σατανᾶ πᾶσά ἐστιν ἡ ἁμαρτία, ᾗ
καὶ ἀποτάσσεσθαι ἀναγκαῖον, ὡσεὶ καὶ τύραννόν τις ἀπο-
φυγὼν πάντως που καὶ τὰ τούτου ὅπλα ἀπέφυγε. πᾶσα οὖν
κατ᾽ εἶδος ἁμαρτία ἐγκατείλεκται τοῖς τοῦ διαβόλου ἔργοις.
πλὴν τοῦτο ἴσθι, ὅτι, ὅσα λέγεις, μάλιστα κατ᾽ ἐκείνην τὴν
φρικωδεστάτην ὥραν, ἔγγραφά ἐστιν ἐν τοῖς τοῦ θεοῦ βιβλίοις·
ἐπειδὰν τοίνυν ἐναντίον τι διαπραττόμενος τούτοις ᾖς, ὡς
παραβάτης κριθήσῃ. ἀποτάσσῃ τοίνυν τοῖς ἔργοις τοῦ σατανᾶ,
πάσαις φημὶ πράξεσι καὶ ἐννοίαις παρὰ λόγον γινομέναις.

6. And (3) of all his Pomp

Εἶτα λέγεις· "καὶ πάσῃ τῇ πομπῇ σου." πομπὴ δὲ διαβόλου ἐστὶ θεατρομανίαι καὶ ἱπποδρομίαι, κυνηγεσία καὶ πᾶσα
τοιαύτη ματαιότης, ἧς εὐχόμενος ἐλευθερωθῆναι ὁ ἅγιος τῷ
θεῷ λέγει· ἀπόστρεψον τοὺς ὀφθαλμούς μου τοῦ μὴ

ἰδεῖν ματαιότητα. μὴ περισπούδαστός σοι ἔστω ἡ
θεατρομανία, ἔνθα τὰς ἀσελγείας τῶν μίμων ὄψῃ, ὕβρεσι
πεπραγμένας καὶ πάσῃ ἀσχημοσύνῃ, ἐκτεθηλυσμένων τε
ἀνδρῶν ἐμμανεῖς ὀρχήσεις· μήτε ᾗ τῶν ἐν κυνηγίοις ἑαυτοὺς
θηρίοις ἐκδιδόντων, ἵνα τὴν ἀθλίαν κολακεύσωσι γαστέρα· οἵ,
ἵνα κοιλίαν τροφαῖς θεραπεύσωσιν, αὐτοὶ γαστρὸς ἀτιθάσων
ἀληθῶς τροφὴ γίνονται θηρίων, ἵνα δὲ δικαίως εἴπω, ὑπὲρ
οἰκείου θεοῦ τῆς κοιλίας τὴν ἑαυτῶν ζωὴν κατὰ κρημνῶν
μονομαχοῦσι. φεῦγε καὶ τὰς ἱπποδρομίας, τὸ ἐμμανὲς θέαμα
καὶ ψυχὰς ἐκτραχηλίζον· ταῦτα γὰρ πάντα πομπή ἐστι τοῦ
διαβόλου.

7. The Meaning of Satan's Pomp

Ἀλλὰ καὶ τὰ ἐν εἰδωλικαῖς πανηγύρεσι κρεμώμενα, ἔσθ᾽ ὅτε
κρέα ἢ ἄρτοι ἢ ἄλλα τοιαῦτα, μιανθέντα τῇ τῶν παμμιάρων
ἐπικλήσει δαιμόνων, τῇ τοῦ διαβόλου πομπῇ ἐγκαταλέγεται.
ὥσπερ γὰρ ὁ ἄρτος καὶ ὁ οἶνος τῆς εὐχαριστίας πρὸ τῆς ἁγίας
ἐπικλήσεως καὶ προσκυνητῆς τριάδος ἄρτος ἦν καὶ οἶνος λιτός,
ἐπικλήσεως δὲ γενομένης ὁ μὲν ἄρτος γίνεται σῶμα Χριστοῦ,
ὁ δὲ οἶνος αἷμα Χριστοῦ, τὸν αὐτὸν δὴ τρόπον τὰ τοιαῦτα
βρώματα τῆς πομπῆς τοῦ σατανᾶ, τῇ ἰδίᾳ φύσει λιτὰ ὄντα, τῇ
ἐπικλήσει τῶν δαιμόνων βέβηλα γίνεται.

8. And (4) of his Cultus

Μετὰ ταῦτα λέγεις· " καὶ πάσῃ τῇ λατρείᾳ σου." λατρεία
δέ ἐστι διαβόλου ἡ ἐν εἰδωλείοις εὐχή, τὰ πρὸς τιμὴν γινόμενα
τῶν ἀψύχων εἰδώλων, τὸ ἅπτειν λύχνους ἢ θυμιᾶν παρὰ πηγὰς
ἢ ποταμούς, ὥς τινες ἀπ᾽ ὀνειράτων ἢ ἐκ δαιμόνων ἀπατη-
θέντες ἐπὶ τούτους διέβησαν, οἰόμενοι καὶ σωματικῶν παθῶν
τὴν ἴασιν εὑρήσειν, ἢ τοιαῦτα· μὴ τοίνυν αὐτὰ μετέλθῃς.

οἰωνοσκοπία, μαντεία, κληδονισμοὶ ἢ περιάμματα ἢ ἐν πετά-
λοις ἐπιγραφαί, μαγεῖαι ἢ ἄλλαι κακοτεχνίαι καὶ ὅσα τοιαῦτα,
λατρεῖαί εἰσι διαβόλου. φεῦγε οὖν ταῦτα· ἐὰν γὰρ τούτοις
ὑποπέσῃς μετὰ τὴν ἀπόταξιν τοῦ σατανᾶ καὶ τὴν πρὸς τὸν
Χριστὸν σύνταξιν, πικροτέρου πειρασθήσῃ τοῦ τυράννου, ἴσως
ὡς οἰκεῖον περιέποντος πάλαι καὶ τῆς πικρᾶς ἀνιέντος σε
δουλείας, νῦν δὲ σφόδρα παρὰ σοῦ καταπικρανθέντος· καὶ τοῦ
Χριστοῦ στερηθήσῃ κἀκείνου περιασθήσῃ.

Οὐκ ἤκουσας παλαιᾶς ἱστορίας τὰ περὶ τοῦ Λὼτ ἡμῖν καὶ
τῶν τούτου θυγατέρων διηγουμένης; οὐχὶ αὐτὸς μὲν σέσωσται
μετὰ τῶν θυγατέρων, ἐπειδὴ τὸ ὄρος κατείληφεν, ἡ δὲ τούτου
γυνὴ στήλη γέγονεν ἁλός, ἐστηλιτευμένη δι᾽ αἰῶνος, ἔχουσα
τῆς πονηρᾶς προαιρέσεως καὶ ὑποστροφῆς τὴν μνήμην;
πρόσεχε τοίνυν σεαυτῷ, καὶ μὴ στρέφου πάλιν εἰς τὰ ὀπίσω,
βαλὼν τὴν χεῖρα ἐπ᾽ ἄροτρον καὶ στρέφων πάλιν εἰς τὴν
ἁλμυρὰν τοῦ βίου τούτου πρᾶξιν· ἀλλὰ φεῦγε εἰς τὸ ὄρος πρὸς
Ἰησοῦν Χριστόν, τὸν τμηθέντα λίθον ἄνευ χειρῶν καὶ τὴν
οἰκουμένην πληρώσαντα.

9. *The Opening of Paradise that ensues*

Ὅτε οὖν τῷ σατανᾷ ἀποτάττῃ, πᾶσαν τὴν πρὸς αὐτὸν
πατῶν διαθήκην, λύεις τὰς παλαιὰς πρὸς τὸν ᾅδην συνθήκας,
ἀνοίγεταί σοι ὁ παράδεισος τοῦ θεοῦ, ὃν ἐφύτευσε κατὰ
ἀνατολάς, ὅθεν διὰ τὴν παράβασιν ἐξόριστος γέγονεν ὁ
ἡμέτερος προπάτωρ. καὶ τούτου σύμβολον τὸ στραφῆναί σε
ἀπὸ δυσμῶν πρὸς ἀνατολήν, τοῦ φωτὸς τὸ χωρίον. τότε σοι
ἐλέγετο εἰπεῖν· "πιστεύω εἰς τὸν πατέρα καὶ εἰς τὸν υἱὸν καὶ
εἰς τὸ ἅγιον πνεῦμα καὶ εἰς ἓν βάπτισμα μετανοίας." περὶ ὧν
ἐν ταῖς προτέραις κατηχήσεσιν, ὡς ἡ τοῦ θεοῦ χάρις ἔδωκεν,
ἐν πλάτει σοι εἴρηται.

10. *The accompanying Joy*

Τούτοις οὖν ἀσφαλιζόμενος τοῖς λόγοις νῆφε. ὁ γὰρ ἀντί-
δικος ἡμῶν διάβολος, καθὼς ἀρτίως ἀνέγνωσται, ὡς λέων
ὠρυόμενος περιπατεῖ, ζητῶν, τίνα καταπίῃ. ἀλλ᾽ ἐν μὲν τοῖς
πρὸ τούτου χρόνοις κατέπιεν ὁ θάνατος ἰσχύσας· ἐπὶ δὲ τοῦ
ἁγίου τῆς παλιγγενεσίας λουτροῦ ἀφεῖλεν ὁ θεὸς πᾶν δάκρυον
ἀπὸ παντὸς προσώπου. οὐκ ἔτι γὰρ πενθήσεις, ἐκδεδυμένος
τὸν παλαιὸν ἄνθρωπον, ἀλλὰ πανηγυρίσεις, ἐνδεδυμένος τὸ
ἱμάτιον σωτηρίου Ἰησοῦν Χριστόν.

11. *The Entry into the Holy of Holies*

Καὶ ταῦτα ἐν τῷ ἐξωτέρῳ ἐγίνετο οἴκῳ. θεοῦ δὲ θέλοντος,
ὅταν ἐν ταῖς ἑξῆς μυσταγωγίαις εἰς τὰ ἅγια τῶν ἁγίων
εἰσέλθωμεν, ἐκεῖ εἰσόμεθα τῶν αὐτόθι ἐπιτελουμένων τὰ
σύμβολα. τῷ δὲ θεῷ πατρὶ ἡ δόξα, κράτος, μεγαλωσύνη σὺν
υἱῷ καὶ ἁγίῳ πνεύματι, εἰς τοὺς αἰῶνας τῶν αἰώνων· ἀμήν.

LECTURE II
THE BAPTISMAL RITE

Καὶ ἀνάγνωσις ἐκ τῆς πρὸς Ῥωμαίους ἐπιστολῆς ἀπὸ τοῦ
ἢ ἀγνοεῖτε ὅτι ὅσοι ἐβαπτίσθημεν εἰς Χριστὸν
Ἰησοῦν εἰς τὸν θάνατον αὐτοῦ ἐβαπτίσθημεν ἕως
τοῦ οὐ γάρ ἐστε ὑπὸ νόμον, ἀλλ᾽ ὑπὸ χάριν·

1. *The Sequel to the last Lecture*

Χρήσιμαι ἡμῖν αἱ καθ᾽ ἡμέραν μυσταγωγίαι καὶ διδασκα-
λίαι καινότεραι, καινοτέρων οὖσαι πραγμάτων ἀπαγγελτικαί,

καὶ μάλιστα ὑμῖν, τοῖς ἀνακαινισθεῖσιν ἀπὸ παλαιότητος
εἰς καινότητα. διὰ τοῦτο ἀναγκαίως ὑμῖν παραθήσομαι τὰ
ἑξῆς τῆς χθεσινῆς μυσταγωγίας, ἵνα μάθητε, τίνων ἦν σύμβολα τὰ ὑφ᾽ ὑμῶν ἐν τῷ ἐσωτέρῳ οἴκῳ γενόμενα.

2. Why the Baptized put off their Garments

Εὐθὺς οὖν εἰσελθόντες ἀπεδύεσθε τὸν χιτῶνα· καὶ τοῦτο ἦν
εἰκὼν τοῦ τὸν παλαιὸν ἄνθρωπον ἀποδύεσθαι σὺν ταῖς πράξε-
σιν. ἀποδυθέντες γυμνοὶ ἦτε, μιμούμενοι καὶ ἐν τούτῳ τὸν
ἐπὶ σταυροῦ γυμνωθέντα Χριστόν, καὶ τῇ γυμνότητι ἀπεκδυ-
σάμενον τὰς ἀρχὰς καὶ τὰς ἐξουσίας, καὶ μετὰ παρρησίας ἐν
τῷ ξύλῳ θριαμβεύσαντα. ἐπειδὴ γὰρ τοῖς μέλεσι τοῖς
ὑμετέροις ἐνεφώλευον αἱ ἀντικείμεναι δυνάμεις, οὐκ ἔτι
φορεῖν ὑμῖν ἔξεστι τὸν παλαιὸν ἐκεῖνον χιτῶνα, οὐ τοῦτον
πάντως λέγω τὸν αἰσθητόν, ἀλλὰ τὸν παλαιὸν ἄνθρωπον τὸν
φθειρόμενον ἐν ταῖς ἐπιθυμίαις τῆς ἀπάτης. ὃν μὴ εἴη πάλιν
ἐνδύσασθαι τῇ ἅπαξ τοῦτον ἀποδυσαμένῃ ψυχῇ, ἀλλὰ λέγειν
κατὰ τὴν ἐν τῷ ᾄσματι τῶν ᾀσμάτων τοῦ Χριστοῦ νύμφην·
ἐξεδυσάμην τὸν χιτῶνά μου, πῶς ἐνδύσομαι αὐτόν;
ὦ θαυμασίου πράγματος· γυμνοὶ ἦτε ἐν ὄψεσι πάντων καὶ
οὐκ ᾐσχύνεσθε. ἀληθῶς γὰρ μίμημα ἐφέρετε τοῦ πρωτο-
πλάστου Ἀδάμ, ὃς ἐν τῷ παραδείσῳ γυμνὸς ἦν καὶ οὐκ
ᾐσχύνετο.

3. The Anointing with Oil

Εἶτα ἀποδυθέντες ἐλαίῳ ἠλείφεσθε ἐπορκιστῷ ἀπ᾽ ἄκρων
τριχῶν κορυφῆς ἕως τῶν κάτω, καὶ κοινωνοὶ ἐγίνεσθε τῆς
καλλιελαίου Ἰησοῦ Χριστοῦ. ἐκκοπέντες γὰρ ἐκ τῆς ἀγριε-
λαίου ἐνεκεντρίζεσθε εἰς τὴν καλλιέλαιον καὶ κοινωνοὶ ἐγίνεσθε

τῆς πιότητος τῆς ἀληθινῆς ἐλαίας. τὸ οὖν ἐπορκιστὸν ἔλαιον
σύμβολον ἦν τῆς κοινωνίας τῆς πιότητος τοῦ Χριστοῦ, φυγαδευτήριον τυγχάνον παντὸς ἴχνους ἀντικειμένης ἐνεργείας.
ὥσπερ γὰρ τὰ ἐμφυσήματα τῶν ἁγίων καὶ ἡ τοῦ ὀνόματος τοῦ
θεοῦ ἐπίκλησις ὥσπερ σφοδροτάτη φλὸξ καίει καὶ ἐκδιώκει
δαίμονας, οὕτω καὶ τὸ ἐπορκιστὸν τοῦτο ἔλαιον ἐπικλήσει
θεοῦ καὶ εὐχῇ δύναμιν τηλικαύτην λαμβάνει, ὥστε οὐ μόνον
καῖον τὰ ἴχνη τῶν ἁμαρτημάτων ἀποκαθαίρειν, ἀλλὰ καὶ
πάσας ἀοράτους τοῦ πονηροῦ ἐκδιώκειν τὰς δυνάμεις.

4. The Baptismal Cleansing

Μετὰ ταῦτα ἐπὶ τὴν ἁγίαν τοῦ θείου βαπτίσματος ἐχειρα-
γωγεῖσθε κολυμβήθραν, ὡς ὁ Χριστὸς ἀπὸ τοῦ σταυροῦ ἐπὶ
τὸ προκείμενον μνῆμα. καὶ ἠρωτᾶτο ἕκαστος, εἰ πιστεύει εἰς
τὸ ὄνομα τοῦ πατρὸς καὶ τοῦ υἱοῦ καὶ τοῦ ἁγίου πνεύματος.
καὶ ὡμολογήσατε τὴν σωτήριον ὁμολογίαν, καὶ κατεδύετε
τρίτον εἰς τὸ ὕδωρ καὶ ἀνεδύετε πάλιν, καὶ ἐνταῦθα διὰ
συμβόλου τὴν τριήμερον τοῦ Χριστοῦ αἰνιττόμενοι ταφήν.
καθάπερ γὰρ ὁ σωτὴρ ἡμῶν τρεῖς ἡμέρας καὶ τρεῖς νύκτας ἐν
τῇ κοιλίᾳ τῆς γῆς ἐποίησεν, οὕτω καὶ ὑμεῖς ἐν τῇ πρώτῃ
ἀναδύσει τὴν πρώτην ἐμμεῖσθε τοῦ Χριστοῦ ἐν τῇ γῇ
ἡμέραν καὶ τῇ καταδύσει τὴν νύκτα· ὥσπερ γὰρ ὁ ἐν νυκτὶ
οὐκέτι βλέπει, ὁ δὲ ἐν ἡμέρᾳ ἐν φωτὶ διάγει, οὕτως ἐν τῇ
καταδύσει ὡς ἐν νυκτὶ οὐδὲν ἑωρᾶτε, ἐν δὲ τῇ ἀναδύσει ὡς
ἐν ἡμέρᾳ ἐτυγχάνετε ὄντες. καὶ ἐν τῷ αὐτῷ ἀπεθνήσκετε καὶ
ἐγεννᾶσθε, καὶ τὸ σωτήριον ἐκεῖνο ὕδωρ καὶ τάφος ὑμῖν
ἐγίνετο καὶ μήτηρ. καὶ ὅπερ Σαλομῶν ἐπὶ ἄλλων εἴρηκε,
τοῦτο ἁρμόσαι ἂν ὑμῖν. ἐκεῖ μὲν γὰρ ἔλεγε· καιρὸς τοῦ
τεκεῖν καὶ καιρὸς τοῦ ἀποθανεῖν· ἐφ᾽ ὑμῖν δὲ τὸ
ἀνάπαλιν· καιρὸς τοῦ ἀποθανεῖν καὶ καιρὸς τοῦ γεννηθῆναι.

καὶ εἷς καιρὸς ἀμφοτέρων τούτων ποιητικός, καὶ σύνδρομος
ἐγίνετο τῷ θανάτῳ ἡ γέννησις ἡ ὑμετέρα.

5. *Mystical Burial and Resurrection with Christ*

῍Ω ξένου καὶ παραδόξου πράγματος· οὐκ ἀληθῶς ἀπεθά-
νομεν, οὐδ' ἀληθῶς ἐτάφημεν, οὐδ' ἀληθῶς σταυρωθέντες
ἀνέστημεν, ἀλλ' ἐν εἰκόνι ἡ μίμησις, ἐν ἀληθείᾳ δὲ ἡ σωτηρία.
Χριστὸς ὄντως ἐσταυρώθη καὶ ὄντως ἐτάφη καὶ ἀληθῶς
ἀνέστη, καὶ πάντα ἡμῖν ταῦτα κεχάρισται, ἵνα τῇ μιμήσει τῶν
παθημάτων αὐτοῦ κοινωνήσαντες ἀληθείᾳ τὴν σωτηρίαν
κερδήσωμεν. ὦ φιλανθρωπίας ὑπερβαλλούσης· Χριστὸς
ἐδέξατο ἐπὶ τῶν ἀχράντων αὐτοῦ χειρῶν καὶ ποδῶν ἥλους καὶ
ἤλγησε, κἀμοὶ ἀναλγητὶ καὶ ἀπονητὶ διὰ τῆς τοῦ ἄλγους
κοινωνίας χαρίζεται τὴν σωτηρίαν.

6. *Wherein Christian Baptism differs from John's*

Μηδεὶς οὖν νομιζέτω τὸ βάπτισμα ἀφέσεως ἁμαρτιῶν
μόνον, ἀλλὰ καὶ υἱοθεσίας χάριν τυγχάνειν, ὡς τὸ Ἰωάννου
ἐτύγχανε βάπτισμα μόνης ἀφέσεως ἁμαρτιῶν παρεκτικόν.
ἀλλ' ἀκριβῶς εἰδότων ἡμῶν, ὅτι ὥς ἐστιν ἁμαρτημάτων
καθαρτήριον καὶ πνεύματος ἁγίου δωρεᾶς πρόξενον, οὕτω καὶ
τῶν τοῦ Χριστοῦ παθημάτων ἀντίτυπον. διὰ τοῦτο γὰρ καὶ
Παῦλος ἀρτίως βοῶν ἔλεγεν· ἢ ἀγνοεῖτε, ὅτι, ὅσοι
ἐβαπτίσθημεν εἰς Χριστὸν Ἰησοῦν, εἰς τὸν θάνατον
αὐτοῦ ἐβαπτίσθημεν; συνετάφημεν οὖν αὐτῷ διὰ
τοῦ βαπτίσματος εἰς τὸν θάνατον. ταῦτα ἔλεγε πρὸς
διατεθέντας, ὡς ἀφέσεως ἁμαρτημάτων καὶ υἱοθεσίας προ-
ξενητικὸν τὸ βάπτισμα, οὐκ ἔτι δὲ καὶ τῶν ἀληθινῶν τοῦ
Χριστοῦ παθημάτων ἐν μιμήσει ἔχει τὴν κοινωνίαν.

7. Salvation through Mystical Participation in Christ's Sufferings

Ἵνα οὖν μάθωμεν, ὅτι, ὅσα ὁ Χριστὸς ὑπέμεινε, δι᾽ ἡμᾶς καὶ τὴν ἡμετέραν σωτηρίαν ἐν ἀληθείᾳ καὶ οὐκ ἐν δοκήσει ταῦτα πέπονθε καὶ ἡμεῖς κοινωνοὶ αὐτοῦ τῶν παθημάτων γινόμεθα, μετὰ πάσης ἐβόα Παῦλος τῆς ἀκριβείας· εἰ γὰρ σύμφυτοι γεγόναμεν τῷ ὁμοιώματι τοῦ θανάτου αὐτοῦ, ἀλλὰ καὶ τῆς ἀναστάσεως ἐσόμεθα. καλῶς δὲ καὶ τὸ " σύμφυτοι "· ἐπειδὴ γὰρ ἐνταῦθα πεφύτευται ἡ ἄμπελος ἡ ἀληθινή, καὶ ἡμεῖς κοινωνίᾳ τοῦ βαπτίσματος τοῦ θανάτου σύμφυτοι αὐτοῦ γεγόναμεν. ἐπίστησον δὲ μετὰ πολλῆς προσοχῆς τὸν νοῦν τοῖς τοῦ ἀποστόλου λόγοις. οὐκ εἶπεν, εἰ γὰρ σύμφυτοι γεγόναμεν τῷ θανάτῳ, ἀλλά, τῷ ὁμοιώματι τοῦ θανάτου. ἀληθῶς γὰρ ἐπὶ Χριστοῦ θάνα-τος, ἀληθῶς γὰρ ἐχωρίζετο τοῦ σώματος ἡ ψυχή· καὶ ἀληθινὴ ταφή, ἐν σινδόνι γὰρ καθαρᾷ τὸ ἅγιον αὐτοῦ σῶμα εἱλεῖτο, καὶ πάντα ἀληθῶς ἐν αὐτῷ συνέβαινεν. ἐπὶ δὲ ὑμῶν θανάτου μὲν καὶ παθημάτων ὁμοίωμα, σωτηρίας δὲ οὐχ ὁμοίωμα, ἀλλὰ ἀλήθεια.

8. The resulting Newness of Life

Ταῦτα διδαχθέντες αὐτάρκως κατέχετε διὰ τῆς μνήμης παρακαλῶ, ἵνα κἀγὼ ὁ ἀνάξιος ἐπὶ ὑμῶν λέγω· ἀγαπῶ δὲ ὑμᾶς, ὅτι πάντοτέ μου μέμνησθε καὶ τὰς παρα-δόσεις, ἃς παρέδωκα ὑμῖν, κατέχετε. δυνατὸς δέ ἐστιν ὁ θεός, ὁ παραστήσας ὑμᾶς ὡς ἐκ νεκρῶν ζῶντας, δοῦναι ὑμῖν ἐν καινότητι ζωῆς περιπατεῖν· ὅτι αὐτῷ ἡ δόξα καὶ τὸ κράτος νῦν καὶ εἰς τοὺς αἰῶνας. ἀμήν.

LECTURE III

THE BAPTISMAL UNCTION

Καὶ ἀνάγνωσις ἐκ τῆς Ἰωάννου καθολικῆς πρώτης ἐπιστολῆς
ἀπὸ τοῦ καὶ ὑμεῖς χρῖσμα ἔχετε ἀπὸ τοῦ θεοῦ καὶ
οἴδατε πάντα, ἕως τοῦ καὶ μὴ αἰσχυνθῶμεν ἀπ᾽
αὐτοῦ ἐπὶ τῇ παρουσίᾳ αὐτοῦ.

1. The Meaning of the Baptismal Unction

Εἰς Χριστὸν βεβαπτισμένοι καὶ Χριστὸν ἐνδυσάμενοι σύμ-
μορφοι γεγόνατε τοῦ υἱοῦ τοῦ θεοῦ. προορίσας γὰρ ἡμᾶς
ὁ θεὸς εἰς υἱοθεσίαν, συμμόρφους ἐποίησε τοῦ σώματος τῆς
δόξης τοῦ Χριστοῦ· μέτοχοι οὖν τοῦ Χριστοῦ γενόμενοι
χριστοὶ εἰκότως καλεῖσθε, καὶ περὶ ὑμῶν ἔλεγεν ὁ θεός· μὴ
ἅψασθε τῶν χριστῶν μου. Χριστοὶ δὲ γεγόνατε τοῦ
ἁγίου πνεύματος τὸ ἀντίτυπον δεξάμενοι, καὶ πάντα εἰκονικῶς
ἐφ᾽ ὑμῶν γεγένηται, ἐπειδὴ εἰκόνες ἐστὲ Χριστοῦ.

Κἀκεῖνος μὲν ἐν Ἰορδάνῃ λουσάμενος ποταμῷ καὶ τῶν
χρώτων τῆς θεότητος μεταδοὺς τοῖς ὕδασιν ἀνέβαινεν ἐκ
τούτων, καὶ πνεύματος ἁγίου οὐσιώδης ἐπιφοίτησις αὐτῷ
ἐγίνετο, τῷ ὁμοίῳ ἐπαναπαυομένου τοῦ ὁμοίου. καὶ ὑμῖν
ὁμοίως ἀναβεβηκόσιν ἀπὸ τῆς κολυμβήθρας τῶν ἱερῶν
ναμάτων ἐδόθη χρῖσμα, τὸ ἀντίτυπον οὗ ἐχρίσθη Χριστός.
τοῦτο δέ ἐστι τὸ ἅγιον πνεῦμα, περὶ οὗ καὶ ὁ μακάριος
Ἡσαΐας ἐν τῇ κατ᾽ αὐτὸν προφητείᾳ ἐκ προσώπου τοῦ
κυρίου ἔλεγε· πνεῦμα κυρίου ἐπ᾽ ἐμέ, οὗ εἵνεκεν
ἔχρισέ με, εὐαγγελίσασθαι πτωχοῖς ἀπέσταλκέ
με.

2. The Spiritual Joy of Unction with the Holy Ghost

Ἐλαίῳ γὰρ ἢ μύρῳ σωματικῷ Χριστὸς ὑπ' ἀνθρώπων οὐκ
ἐχρίσθη, ἀλλ' ὁ πατὴρ αὐτὸν σωτῆρα προχειρισάμενος τοῦ
παντὸς κόσμου πνεύματι ἔχρισεν ἁγίῳ, ὡς Πέτρος φησίν·
Ἰησοῦν τὸν ἀπὸ Ναζαρέτ, ὃν ἔχρισεν ὁ θεὸς πνεύματι ἁγίῳ. καὶ ὁ Δαβὶδ ὁ προφήτης ἐβόα λέγων· ὁ θρόνος
σου ὁ θεὸς εἰς τὸν αἰῶνα τοῦ αἰῶνος· ῥάβδος
εὐθύτητος ἡ ῥάβδος τῆς βασιλείας σου. ἠγάπησας
δικαιοσύνην καὶ ἐμίσησας ἀδικίαν· διὰ τοῦτο
ἔχρισέ σε ὁ θεός, ὁ θεός σου, ἔλαιον ἀγαλλιάσεως
παρὰ τοὺς μετόχους σου.

Καὶ ὥσπερ ὁ Χριστὸς ἀληθῶς ἐσταυροῦτο καὶ ἐθάπτετο
καὶ ἠγείρετο, ὑμεῖς δὲ κατὰ τὸ βάπτισμα ἐν ὁμοιώματι καὶ
συσταυρωθῆναι καὶ συνταφῆναι καὶ συναναστῆναι αὐτῷ κατ-
αξιοῦσθε, οὕτω καὶ ἐπὶ τοῦ χρίσματος. ἐκεῖνος ἐλαίῳ νοητῷ
ἀγαλλιάσεως ἐχρίετο, τουτέστι πνεύματι ἁγίῳ, ἀγαλλιάσεως
καλουμένῳ διὰ τὸ αἴτιον αὐτὸ τῆς πνευματικῆς τυγχάνειν
ἀγαλλιάσεως· ὑμεῖς δὲ μύρῳ ἐχρίσθητε, κοινωνοὶ καὶ μέτοχοι
τοῦ Χριστοῦ γενόμενοι.

3. The Sanctifying Power of the Holy Ghost

Ἀλλ' ὅρα μὴ ὑπονοήσῃς ἐκεῖνο τὸ μύρον ψιλὸν εἶναι. ὥσπερ
γὰρ ὁ ἄρτος τῆς εὐχαριστίας μετὰ τὴν ἐπίκλησιν τοῦ ἁγίου
πνεύματος οὐκ ἔτι ἄρτος λιτός, ἀλλὰ σῶμα Χριστοῦ, οὕτω
καὶ τὸ ἅγιον τοῦτο μύρον οὐκ ἔτι ψιλὸν οὐδ' ὡς ἂν εἴποι τις
κοινὸν μετ' ἐπίκλησιν, ἀλλὰ Χριστοῦ χάρισμα καὶ πνεύματος
ἁγίου παρουσίᾳ τῆς αὐτοῦ θεότητος ἐνεργητικὸν γινόμενον.
ὅπερ συμβολικῶς ἐπὶ μετώπου καὶ τῶν ἄλλων σου χρίεται
αἰσθητηρίων. καὶ τῷ μὲν φαινομένῳ μύρῳ τὸ σῶμα χρίεται,
τῷ δὲ ἁγίῳ καὶ ἀοράτῳ πνεύματι ἡ ψυχὴ ἁγιάζεται.

4. *The Method of Unction*

Καὶ πρῶτον ἐχρίεσθε ἐπὶ τὸ μέτωπον, ἵνα ἀπαλλαγῆτε τῆς
αἰσχύνης, ἣν ὁ πρῶτος παραβάτης ἄνθρωπος πανταχοῦ
περιέφερε, καὶ ἵνα ἀνακεκαλυμμένῳ προσώπῳ τὴν δόξαν
κυρίου κατοπτρίζησθε. εἶτα ἐπὶ τὰ ὦτα, ἵνα προσλάβητε τὰ
ἀκουστικὰ τῶν θείων μυστηρίων ὦτα, περὶ ὧν Ἡσαΐας
ἔλεγε· καὶ προσέθηκέ μοι κύριος ὠτίον τοῦ ἀκούειν,
καὶ ὁ κύριος Ἰησοῦς ἐν εὐαγγελίοις· ὁ ἔχων ὦτα ἀκούειν
ἀκουέτω. εἶτα ἐπὶ τὴν ὄσφρησιν, ὅπως τοῦ θείου ἀντι-
λαμβανόμενοι μύρου λέγητε· Χριστοῦ εὐωδία ἐσμὲν τῷ
θεῷ ἐν τοῖς σῳζομένοις. μετὰ ταῦτα ἐπὶ τὰ στήθη ἵνα
ἐνδυσάμενοι τὸν θώρακα τῆς δικαιοσύνης στῆτε
πρὸς τὰς μεθοδείας τοῦ διαβόλου. ὥσπερ γὰρ ὁ
Χριστὸς μετὰ τὸ βάπτισμα καὶ τὴν τοῦ ἁγίου πνεύματος
ἐπιφοίτησιν ἐξελθὼν κατηγωνίσατο τὸν ἀντικείμενον, οὕτω
καὶ ὑμεῖς μετὰ τὸ ἱερὸν βάπτισμα καὶ τὸ μυστικὸν χρῖσμα
ἐνδεδυμένοι τὴν πανοπλίαν τοῦ ἁγίου πνεύματος ἵστασθε πρὸς
τὴν ἀντικειμένην δύναμιν καὶ ταύτην καταγωνίζεσθε, λέγοντες·
πάντα ἰσχύω ἐν τῷ ἐνδυναμοῦντί με Χριστῷ.

5. *Unction and the Christian Name*

Τούτου τοῦ ἁγίου χρίσματος καταξιωθέντες καλεῖσθε
χριστιανοί, ἐπαληθεύοντες τῇ ἀναγεννήσει καὶ τὸ ὄνομα. πρὸ
γὰρ τοῦ καταξιωθῆναι ὑμᾶς ταύτης τῆς χάριτος, ταύτης τῆς
προσηγορίας κυρίως οὐκ ἦτε ἄξιοι, ἀλλ’ ὁδεύοντες προεβαίνετε
εἰς τὸ εἶναι χριστιανοί.

6. *The Foreshadowing of Christian Unction*

Εἰδέναι δὲ ὑμᾶς ἀναγκαῖον, ὅτι τοῦ χρίσματος τούτου ἐν
τῇ παλαιᾷ γραφῇ τὸ σύμβολον κεῖται. καὶ γὰρ ὁπηνίκα τὸ

τοῦ θεοῦ πρόσταγμα Μωσῆς τῷ ἀδελφῷ μετεδίδου, ἀρχιερέα καθιστῶν τοῦτον, μετὰ τὸ ἐν ὕδατι λούσασθαι ἔχρισε, καὶ ἐκαλεῖτο χριστὸς ἐκ τοῦ χρίσματος δηλαδὴ τοῦ τυπικοῦ. οὕτω καὶ τὸν Σολομῶνα προάγων εἰς βασιλέα, ἔχρισεν αὐτὸν μετὰ τὸ λούσασθαι ἐν τῷ Γειὼν ὁ ἀρχιερεύς. ἀλλὰ ταῦτα μὲν ἐκείνοις συνέβαινε τυπικῶς, ὑμῖν δὲ οὐ τυπικῶς ἀλλ' ἀληθῶς, ἐπειδὴ ἀπὸ τοῦ ἁγίου πνεύματος ἐχρίεσθε ἀληθῶς. ἡ ἀρχὴ τῆς ὑμετέρας σωτηρίας ὁ Χριστός· ἐκεῖνος γὰρ ἀληθῶς ἀπαρχή, καὶ ὑμεῖς τὸ φύραμα· εἰ δὲ ἡ ἀπαρχὴ ἁγία, δῆλον ὅτι μεταβήσεται ἐπὶ τὸ φύραμα ἡ ἁγιότης.

7. The Power of Unction to safeguard the Soul

Τοῦτο φυλάξατε ἄσπιλον· πάντων γὰρ ἔσται τοῦτο διδακτικόν, εἰ ἐν ὑμῖν μένοι, καθὼς ἀρτίως ἠκούσατε τοῦ μακαρίου Ἰωάννου λέγοντος καὶ πολλὰ περὶ τοῦ χρίσματος φιλοσοφοῦντος. ἔστι γὰρ τοῦτο τὸ ἅγιον πνευματικὸν σώματος φυλακτήριον καὶ ψυχῆς σωτήριον.

Τοῦτο ἐκ παλαιῶν χρόνων ὁ μακάριος Ἡσαΐας προφητεύων ἔλεγε· καὶ ποιήσει κύριος πᾶσιν ἔθνεσιν ἐπὶ τὸ ὄρος τοῦτο (ὄρος δὲ καλεῖ τὴν ἐκκλησίαν, καὶ ἀλλαχοῦ, ὡς ὅταν λέγῃ· καὶ ἔσται ἐν ταῖς ἐσχάταις ἡμέραις ἐμφανὲς τὸ ὄρος κυρίου), πίονται οἶνον, πίονται εὐφροσύνην, χρίσονται μύρον. καὶ ἵνα ἀσφαλίσηταί σε, ἄκουε ἃ περὶ τούτου τοῦ μύρου ὡς μυστικοῦ φησι· παράδος ταῦτα πάντα τοῖς ἔθνεσιν· ἡ γὰρ βουλὴ τοῦ κυρίου ἐπὶ πάντα τὰ ἔθνη.

Τούτῳ οὖν χρισθέντες τῷ ἁγίῳ μύρῳ τηρήσατε αὐτὸ ἄσπιλον καὶ ἄμωμον ἐν ὑμῖν, δι' ἔργων ἀγαθῶν προκόπτοντες καὶ εὐάρεστοι γινόμενοι τῷ ἀρχηγῷ τῆς σωτηρίας ὑμῶν Χριστῷ Ἰησοῦ, ᾧ ἡ δόξα εἰς τοὺς αἰῶνας τῶν αἰώνων. ἀμήν.

LECTURE IV

THE EUCHARIST

Καὶ ἀνάγνωσις ἐκ τῆς πρὸς Κορινθίους Παύλου ἐπιστολῆς·
Ἐγὼ γὰρ παρέλαβον ἀπὸ τοῦ κυρίου, ὃ καὶ παρέδωκα ὑμῖν καὶ τὰ ἑξῆς.

1. The Teaching of St. Paul

Καὶ αὕτη τοῦ μακαρίου Παύλου ἡ διδασκαλία ἱκανὴ
καθέστηκε πληροφορῆσαι ὑμᾶς περὶ τῶν θείων μυστηρίων,
ὧν καταξιωθέντες σύσσωμοι καὶ σύναιμοι τοῦ Χριστοῦ
γεγόνατε. αὐτὸς γὰρ ἀρτίως ἐβόα· ὅτι ἐν τῇ νυκτὶ ᾗ
παρεδίδοτο ὁ κύριος ἡμῶν Ἰησοῦς Χριστός,
λαβὼν ἄρτον καὶ εὐχαριστήσας ἔκλασε καὶ ἔδωκε
τοῖς ἑαυτοῦ μαθηταῖς λέγων· λάβετε, φάγετε,
τοῦτό μού ἐστι τὸ σῶμα. καὶ λαβὼν τὸ ποτήριον
καὶ εὐχαριστήσας εἶπε· λάβετε, πίετε, τοῦτό μού
ἐστι τὸ αἷμα. αὐτοῦ οὖν ἀποφηναμένου καὶ εἰπόντος περὶ
τοῦ ἄρτου " τοῦτό μού ἐστι τὸ σῶμα ", τίς τολμήσει ἀμφι-
βάλλειν λοιπόν; καὶ αὐτοῦ βεβαιωσαμένου καὶ εἰρηκότος
" τοῦτό μού ἐστι τὸ αἷμα ", τίς ἐνδοιάσει ποτὲ λέγων μὴ
εἶναι αὐτοῦ τὸ αἷμα;

2. The Parallel Miracle at Cana of Galilee

Τὸ ὕδωρ ποτὲ εἰς οἶνον οἰκείῳ νεύματι μεταβέβληκεν ἐν
Κανᾷ τῆς Γαλιλαίας, καὶ οὐκ ἀξιόπιστός ἐστιν οἶνον μετα-
βαλὼν εἰς αἷμα; εἰς γάμον σωματικὸν κληθεὶς ταύτην ἐθαυ-
ματούργησε τὴν παραδοξοποιΐαν, καὶ τοῖς υἱοῖς τοῦ νυμφῶνος

οὐ πολλῷ μᾶλλον τὴν ἀπόλαυσιν τοῦ σώματος αὐτοῦ καὶ τοῦ
αἵματος δωρησάμενος ὁμολογηθήσεται;

3. The Partaking of Christ in the Eucharist

Ὥστε μετὰ πάσης πληροφορίας ὡς σώματος καὶ αἵματος
μεταλαμβάνωμεν Χριστοῦ. ἐν τύπῳ γὰρ ἄρτου δίδοταί σοι
τὸ σῶμα, καὶ ἐν τύπῳ οἴνου δίδοταί σοι τὸ αἷμα, ἵνα γένῃ,
μεταλαβὼν σώματος καὶ αἵματος Χριστοῦ, σύσσωμος καὶ
σύναιμος αὐτοῦ. οὕτω γὰρ καὶ χριστοφόροι γινόμεθα, τοῦ
σώματος αὐτοῦ καὶ τοῦ αἵματος εἰς τὰ ἡμέτερα ἀναδιδομένου
μέλη. οὕτω κατὰ τὸν μακάριον Πέτρον θείας κοινωνοὶ
φύσεως γινόμεθα.

4. Spiritual Food and Drink

Ποτὲ Χριστὸς τοῖς Ἰουδαίοις διαλεγόμενος ἔλεγεν· ἐὰν
μὴ φάγητέ μου τὴν σάρκα καὶ πίητέ μου τὸ αἷμα,
οὐκ ἔχετε ζωὴν ἐν ἑαυτοῖς. ἐκεῖνοι, μὴ ἀκηκοότες
πνευματικῶς τῶν λεγομένων, σκανδαλισθέντες ἀπῆλθον εἰς
τὰ ὀπίσω, νομίζοντες ὅτι ἐπὶ σαρκοφαγίαν αὐτοὺς προτρέ-
πεται.

5. The Bread of Heaven and the Cup of Salvation

Ἦσαν καὶ ἐν παλαιᾷ διαθήκῃ ἄρτοι προθέσεως· ἀλλ'
ἐκεῖνοι παλαιᾶς ὄντες διαθήκης τέλος εἰλήφασιν. ἐν δὲ τῇ
καινῇ διαθήκῃ ἄρτος οὐράνιος καὶ ποτήριον σωτηρίου, ψυχὴν
καὶ σῶμα ἁγιάζοντα· ὥσπερ γὰρ ὁ ἄρτος σώματι κατάλληλος,
οὕτω καὶ ὁ λόγος τῇ ψυχῇ ἁρμόδιος.

6. Verily the Body and Blood of Christ

Μὴ πρόσεχε οὖν ὡς ψιλοῖς τῷ ἄρτῳ καὶ τῷ οἴνῳ· σῶμα γὰρ
καὶ αἷμα Χριστοῦ κατὰ τὴν δεσποτικὴν τυγχάνει ἀπόφασιν.

εἰ γὰρ καὶ ἡ αἴσθησίς σοι τοῦτο ὑποβάλλει, ἀλλὰ ἡ πίστις σε βεβαιούτω. μὴ ἀπὸ τῆς γεύσεως κρίνῃς τὸ πρᾶγμα, ἀλλ' ἀπὸ τῆς πίστεως πληροφοροῦ ἀνενδοιάστως σώματος καὶ αἵματος Χριστοῦ καταξιωθείς.

7. The Table foretold by David

Καὶ ὑπαγορεύσει σοι Δαβὶδ ὁ μακάριος τὴν δύναμιν, λέγων· ἡτοίμασας ἐνώπιόν μου τράπεζαν ἐξεναντίας τῶν θλιβόντων με. ὁ δὲ λέγει, τοιοῦτόν ἐστι. πρὸ τῆς σῆς παρουσίας τράπεζαν οἱ δαίμονες τοῖς ἀνθρώποις ἡτοίμασαν, ἠλισγημένην καὶ μεμιασμένην καὶ διαβολικῆς πεπληρωμένην δυνάμεως· ἀλλὰ μετὰ τὴν σὴν παρουσίαν, ὦ δέσποτα, ἡτοίμασας ἐνώπιόν μου τράπεζαν. ὅταν ὁ ἄνθρωπος λέγῃ θεῷ ἡτοίμασας ἐνώπιόν μου τράπεζαν, τί ἄλλο σημαίνει ἢ τὴν μυστικὴν καὶ νοητὴν τράπεζαν, ἣν ὁ θεὸς ἡμῖν ἡτοίμασεν ἐξεναντίας, ἀντὶ τοῦ ἐκ τοῦ ἐναντίου καὶ ἀντικειμένως τοῖς δαίμοσιν; καὶ μάλα εἰκότως· ἐκείνη μὲν γὰρ κοινωνίαν ἔσχε δαιμόνων, αὕτη δὲ κοινωνίαν θεοῦ. ἐλίπανας ἐν ἐλαίῳ τὴν κεφαλήν μου. ἐλαίῳ ἐλίπανέ σου τὴν κεφαλὴν ἐπὶ μετώπου διὰ τὴν σφραγῖδα, ἣν ἔχεις τοῦ θεοῦ, ἵνα γένῃ ἐκτύπωμα σφραγῖδος, ἁγίασμα θεοῦ. καὶ τὸ ποτήριόν σου μεθύσκον με ὡσεὶ κράτιστον. ὁρᾷς ἐνταῦθα ποτήριον λεγόμενον, ὃ λαβὼν Ἰησοῦς μετὰ χεῖρας καὶ εὐχαριστήσας εἶπε· τοῦτό μού ἐστι τὸ αἷμα τὸ ὑπὲρ πολλῶν ἐκχυνόμενον εἰς ἄφεσιν ἁμαρτιῶν.

8. Its Delights pointed to by Solomon

Διὰ τοῦτο καὶ ὁ Σολομὼν ταύτην αἰνιττόμενος τὴν χάριν ἐν τῷ Ἐκκλησιαστῇ λέγει· δεῦρο, φάγε ἐν εὐφροσύνῃ τὸν ἄρτον σου, τὸν πνευματικὸν ἄρτον. δεῦρο· καλεῖ τὴν

σωτήριον καὶ μακαριοποιὸν κλῆσιν. καὶ πίε τὸν οἶνόν
σου ἐν καρδίᾳ ἀγαθῇ, τὸν πνευματικὸν οἶνον, καὶ
ἔλαιον ὑπὲρ κεφαλῆς σου ἐκχείσθω· ὁρᾷς αὐτὸν καὶ
τὸ μυστικὸν αἰνιττόμενον χρῖσμα. καὶ διαπαντὸς ἔστω
σου τὰ ἱμάτια λευκά, ὅτι εὐδόκησε κύριος τὰ
ποιήματά σου. πρὶν γὰρ προσέλθῃς τῇ χάριτι, ματαιότης
ματαιοτήτων ἦν τὰ ποιήματά σου.

Ἀποδυσάμενον δὲ τὰ παλαιὰ ἱμάτια καὶ ἐνδυσάμενον τὰ
πνευματικῶς λευκὰ χρὴ λευχειμονεῖν διαπαντός. οὐ πάντως
τοῦτο λέγομεν, ὅτι σε δεῖ λευκὰ ἱμάτια περιβεβλῆσθαι ἀεί,
ἀλλὰ τὰ ὄντως λευκὰ καὶ λαμπρὰ καὶ πνευματικὰ ἀναγκαῖόν
ἐστι περιβεβλῆσθαι, ἵνα λέγῃς κατὰ τὸν μακάριον Ἡσαΐαν·
ἀγαλλιάσθω ἡ ψυχή μου ἐπὶ τῷ κυρίῳ· ἐνέδυσε γάρ
με ἱμάτιον σωτηρίου καὶ χιτῶνα εὐφροσύνης
περιέθηκέ μοι.

9. Its Effects progress from Glory to Glory

Ταῦτα μαθὼν καὶ πληροφορηθείς, ὡς ὁ φαινόμενος ἄρτος
οὐκ ἄρτος ἐστίν, εἰ καὶ τῇ γεύσει αἰσθητός, ἀλλὰ σῶμα
Χριστοῦ, καὶ ὁ φαινόμενος οἶνος οὐκ οἶνός ἐστιν, εἰ καὶ ἡ
γεῦσις τοῦτο βούλεται, ἀλλὰ αἷμα Χριστοῦ, καὶ ὅτι περὶ
τούτου ἔλεγε πάλαι ὁ Δαβὶδ ψάλλων καὶ ἄρτος καρδίαν
ἀνθρώπου στηρίζει, τοῦ ἱλαρῦναι πρόσωπον ἐν
ἐλαίῳ, στηρίζου τὴν καρδίαν, μεταλαμβάνων αὐτοῦ ὡς
πνευματικοῦ, καὶ ἱλάρυνον τὸ τῆς ψυχῆς σου πρόσωπον. ὃ
γένοιτό σε ἀνακεκαλυμμένον ἔχοντα ἐν καθαρᾷ συνειδήσει,
τὴν δόξαν κυρίου κατοπτριζόμενον, ἔρχεσθαι ἀπὸ δόξης εἰς
δόξαν, ἐν Χριστῷ Ἰησοῦ τῷ κυρίῳ ἡμῶν, ᾧ ἡ τιμὴ καὶ
κράτος καὶ δόξα εἰς τοὺς αἰῶνας τῶν αἰώνων. ἀμήν.

Lecture V

THE EUCHARISTIC RITE

Ἐκ τῆς Πέτρου καθολικῆς ἐπιστολῆς· Διὸ ἀποθέμενοι πᾶσαν ῥυπαρίαν καὶ πάντα δόλον καὶ καταλαλιάν, καὶ τὰ ἑξῆς.

1. The Concluding Lecture

Τῇ τοῦ θεοῦ φιλανθρωπίᾳ ἐν ταῖς προλαβούσαις συνάξεσιν ἀρκούντως ἀκηκόατε περί τε βαπτίσματος καὶ χρίσματος καὶ μεταλήψεως σώματος καὶ αἵματος Χριστοῦ. νῦν δὲ ἐπὶ τὰ ἑξῆς μεταβαίνειν ἀναγκαῖον, σήμερον τὴν στεφάνην ἐπιθήσοντας τῇ πνευματικῇ ὑμῶν τῆς ὠφελείας οἰκοδομῇ.

2. Why the Celebrant washes his Hands

Ἑωράκατε τοίνυν τὸν διάκονον τὸν νίψασθαι διδόντα τῷ ἱερεῖ καὶ τοῖς κυκλοῦσι τὸ θυσιαστήριον τοῦ θεοῦ πρεσβυτέροις. οὐ πάντως δὲ ἐδίδου διὰ τὸν σωματικὸν ῥύπον· οὐκ ἔστι τοῦτο· οὐδὲ γὰρ ῥύπον σώματος ἔχοντες τὴν ἀρχὴν εἰσῄειμεν εἰς τὴν ἐκκλησίαν. ἀλλὰ σύμβολόν ἐστι τοῦ δεῖν ὑμᾶς καθαρεύειν πάντων ἁμαρτημάτων καὶ ἀνομημάτων τὸ νίψασθαι. ἐπειδὴ γὰρ αἱ χεῖρες σύμβολον πράξεως, τῷ νίψασθαι ταύτας τὸ καθαρὸν δηλονότι καὶ ἄμωμον τῶν πράξεων αἰνιττόμεθα. οὐκ ἤκουσας τοῦ μακαρίου Δαβὶδ αὐτὸ τοῦτο μυσταγωγοῦντος καὶ λέγοντος· νίψομαι ἐν ἀθῴοις τὰς χεῖράς μου καὶ κυκλώσω τὸ θυσιαστήριόν σου, κύριε; οὐκοῦν τὸ νίψασθαι τὰς χεῖρας τοῦ ἀνυπεύθυνον εἶναι ἁμαρτήμασι σύμβολόν ἐστιν.

3. *The Kiss of Peace*

Εἶτα βοᾷ ὁ διάκονος· "ἀλλήλους ἀπολάβετε καὶ ἀλλήλους ἀσπαζώμεθα." μὴ ὑπολάβῃς τὸ φίλημα ἐκεῖνο σύνηθες εἶναι τοῖς ἐπ᾽ ἀγορᾶς γινομένοις ὑπὸ τῶν κοινῶν φίλων· οὐκ ἔστι τοῦτο τοιοῦτον, ἀλλὰ τὸ φίλημα τοῦτο ἀνακίρνησι τὰς ψυχὰς ἀλλήλαις καὶ πᾶσαν ἀμνησικακίαν αὐταῖς μνηστεύεται. σημεῖον τοίνυν ἐστὶ τὸ φίλημα τοῦ ἀνακραθῆναι τὰς ψυχὰς καὶ πᾶσαν ἐξορίζειν μνησικακίαν. διὰ τοῦτο ὁ Χριστὸς ἔλεγεν· ἐὰν προφέρῃς τὸ δῶρόν σου ἐπὶ τὸ θυσιαστή-ριον καὶ ἐκεῖ μνησθῇς, ὅτι ὁ ἀδελφός σου ἔχει τι κατὰ σοῦ, ἄφες τὸ δῶρόν σου ἐπὶ τὸ θυσιαστήριον καὶ ὕπαγε πρῶτον καὶ διαλλάγηθι τῷ ἀδελφῷ σου, καὶ τότε προσελθὼν πρόσφερε τὸ δῶρόν σου. οὐκοῦν τὸ φίλημα διαλλαγή ἐστι καὶ διὰ τοῦτο ἅγιον, ὥς που ὁ μακάριος Παῦλος ἐβόα λέγων ἀσπάσασθε ἀλλήλους ἐν φιλήματι ἁγίῳ, καὶ Πέτρος· ἐν φιλήματι ἀγάπης.

4. *'Sursum Corda'*

Μετὰ τοῦτο βοᾷ ὁ ἱερεύς· "ἄνω τὰς καρδίας." ἀληθῶς γὰρ κατ᾽ ἐκείνην τὴν φρικωδεστάτην ὥραν δεῖ ἄνω ἔχειν τὴν καρδίαν πρὸς τὸν θεόν, καὶ μὴ κάτω περὶ τὴν γῆν καὶ τὰ γήινα πράγματα. δυνάμει τοίνυν ὁ ἱερεὺς προστάττει κατ᾽ ἐκείνην τὴν ὥραν πάντας ἀφιέναι φροντίδας βιωτικάς, μερίμνας τὰς κατ᾽ οἶκον καὶ ἔχειν ἐν οὐρανῷ τὴν καρδίαν πρὸς τὸν φιλάνθρωπον θεόν.

Εἶτα ἀποκρίνεσθε· "ἔχομεν πρὸς τὸν κύριον", τούτῳ συγκατατιθέμενοι, δι᾽ ὧν ὁμολογεῖτε. μηδεὶς δὲ τοιοῦτος παρέστω, ὡς στόματι μὲν λέγειν "ἔχομεν πρὸς τὸν κύριον", τῇ δὲ διανοίᾳ περὶ τὰς βιωτικὰς ἔχειν τὸν νοῦν φροντίδας. πάντοτε μὲν οὖν θεοῦ μνημονευτέον· εἰ δὲ τοῦτο διὰ τὴν

ἀσθένειαν τὴν ἀνθρωπίνην ἀδύνατον, κατ᾽ ἐκείνην μάλιστα τὴν
ὥραν τοῦτο φιλοτιμητέον.

5. 'Habemus ad Dominum'

Εἶτα ὁ ἱερεὺς λέγει· " εὐχαριστήσωμεν τῷ κυρίῳ·" ὄντως
γὰρ εὐχαριστεῖν ὀφείλομεν, ὅτι ἀναξίους ὄντας ἡμᾶς ἐκάλεσεν
εἰς τὴν τηλικαύτην χάριν, ὅτι ἐχθροὺς ὄντας ἡμᾶς κατήλλαξεν,
ὅτι πνεύματος υἱοθεσίας κατηξίωσεν. εἶτα λέγετε· " ἄξιον καὶ
δίκαιον." εὐχαριστοῦντες γὰρ ἡμεῖς ἄξιον ποιοῦμεν πρᾶγμα
καὶ δίκαιον, αὐτὸς δὲ οὐ δίκαιον, ἀλλ᾽ ὑπὲρ τὸ δίκαιον ποιῶν
ἡμᾶς εὐηργέτησε καὶ τηλικούτων ἠξίωσεν ἀγαθῶν.

6. The Preface

Μετὰ ταῦτα μνημονεύομεν οὐρανοῦ καὶ γῆς καὶ θαλάσσης,
ἡλίου καὶ σελήνης, ἄστρων καὶ πάσης τῆς κτίσεως λογικῆς
τε καὶ ἀλόγου, ὁρατῆς τε καὶ ἀοράτου, ἀγγέλων, ἀρχαγγέλων,
δυνάμεων, κυριοτήτων, ἀρχῶν, ἐξουσιῶν, θρόνων, τῶν
χερουβὶμ τῶν πολυπροσώπων, δυνάμει λέγοντες τὸ τοῦ Δαβίδ·
μεγαλύνατε τὸν κύριον σὺν ἐμοί. μνημονεύομεν καὶ
τῶν σεραφίμ, ἃ ἐν πνεύματι ἁγίῳ ἐθεάσατο Ἡσαΐας παρεστη-
κότα κύκλῳ τοῦ θρόνου τοῦ θεοῦ, καὶ ταῖς μὲν δυσὶ πτέρυξι
κατακαλύπτοντα τὸ πρόσωπον, ταῖς δὲ δυσὶ τοὺς πόδας καὶ
ταῖς δυσὶ πετόμενα, καὶ λέγοντα ἅγιος ἅγιος ἅγιος
κύριος σαβαώθ. διὰ τοῦτο γὰρ τὴν παραδοθεῖσαν ἡμῖν
ἐκ τῶν σεραφὶμ θεολογίαν ταύτην λέγομεν, ὅπως κοινωνοὶ τῆς
ὑμνῳδίας ταῖς ὑπερκοσμίοις γενώμεθα στρατιαῖς.

7. The Epiclesis

Εἶτα ἁγιάσαντες ἑαυτοὺς διὰ τῶν πνευματικῶν τούτων
ὕμνων παρακαλοῦμεν τὸν φιλάνθρωπον θεὸν τὸ ἅγιον πνεῦμα

ἐξαποστεῖλαι ἐπὶ τὰ προκείμενα, ἵνα ποιήσῃ τὸν μὲν ἄρτον σῶμα Χριστοῦ, τὸν δὲ οἶνον αἷμα Χριστοῦ· πάντως γάρ, οὗ ἂν ἐφάψηται τὸ ἅγιον πνεῦμα, τοῦτο ἡγίασται καὶ μεταβέβληται.

8. Intercessions

Εἶτα μετὰ τὸ ἀπαρτισθῆναι τὴν πνευματικὴν θυσίαν, τὴν ἀναίμακτον λατρείαν, ἐπὶ τῆς θυσίας ἐκείνης τοῦ ἱλασμοῦ, παρακαλοῦμεν τὸν θεὸν ὑπὲρ κοινῆς τῶν ἐκκλησιῶν εἰρήνης, ὑπὲρ τῆς τοῦ κόσμου εὐσταθείας, ὑπὲρ βασιλέων, ὑπὲρ στρατιωτῶν καὶ συμμάχων, ὑπὲρ τῶν ἐν ἀσθενείαις, ὑπὲρ τῶν καταπονουμένων, καὶ ἁπαξαπλῶς ὑπὲρ πάντων βοηθείας δεομένων δεόμεθα πάντες ἡμεῖς καὶ ταύτην προσφέρομεν τὴν θυσίαν.

9. Commemoration of the Departed

Εἶτα μνημονεύομεν καὶ τῶν προκεκοιμημένων, πρῶτον πατριαρχῶν, προφητῶν, ἀποστόλων, μαρτύρων, ὅπως ὁ θεὸς ταῖς εὐχαῖς αὐτῶν καὶ πρεσβείαις προσδέξηται ἡμῶν τὴν δέησιν. εἶτα καὶ ὑπὲρ τῶν προκεκοιμημένων ἁγίων πατέρων καὶ ἐπισκόπων καὶ πάντων ἁπλῶς τῶν ἐν ἡμῖν προκεκοιμημένων, μεγίστην ὄνησιν πιστεύοντες ἔπεσθαι ταῖς ψυχαῖς, ὑπὲρ ὧν ἡ δέησις ἀναφέρεται, τῆς ἁγίας καὶ φρικωδεστάτης προκειμένης θυσίας.

10. Prayer for the Departed

Καὶ βούλομαι ὑμᾶς ἀπὸ ὑποδείγματος πεῖσαι. οἶδα γὰρ πολλοὺς τοῦτο λέγοντας· τί ὠφελεῖται ψυχὴ μετὰ ἁμαρτημάτων ἀπαλλασσομένη τοῦδε τοῦ κόσμου ἢ οὐ μεθ' ἁμαρτημάτων, ἐὰν ἐπὶ τῆς προσευχῆς μνημονεύηται; ἆρα γὰρ εἴ τις

βασιλεὺς προσκεκρουκότας αὐτῷ ἐξορίστους ποιήσειεν, εἶτα
οἱ τούτοις διαφέροντες, στέφανον πλέξαντες, ὑπὲρ τῶν ἐν
τιμωρίαις αὐτῷ τοῦτον προσενέγκοιεν, οὐκ ἂν αὐτοῖς ἄνεσιν
δῴη τῶν κολάσεων; τὸν αὐτὸν τρόπον καὶ ἡμεῖς ὑπὲρ τῶν
κεκοιμημένων αὐτῷ τὰς δεήσεις προσφέροντες, κἂν ἁμαρ-
τωλοὶ ὦσιν, οὐ στέφανον πλέκομεν, ἀλλὰ Χριστὸν ἐσφαγια-
σμένον ὑπὲρ τῶν ἡμετέρων ἁμαρτημάτων προσφέρομεν,
ἐξιλεούμενοι ὑπὲρ αὐτῶν τε καὶ ἡμῶν τὸν φιλάνθρωπον θεόν.

11. The 'Paternoster'

Εἶτα μετὰ ταῦτα τὴν εὐχὴν λέγομεν ἐκείνην, ἣν ὁ σωτὴρ
παρέδωκε τοῖς οἰκείοις αὐτοῦ μαθηταῖς, μετὰ καθαρᾶς
συνειδήσεως πατέρα ἐπιγραφόμενοι τὸν θεὸν καὶ λέγοντες·
πάτερ ἡμῶν ὁ ἐν τοῖς οὐρανοῖς. ὦ τῆς μεγίστης τοῦ
θεοῦ φιλανθρωπίας· τοῖς ἀποπηδήσασιν αὐτοῦ καὶ ἐν ἐσχάτοις
γενομένοις κακοῖς τοσαύτην δεδώρηται κακῶν ἀμνηστίαν καὶ
χάριτος μετουσίαν, ὡς καὶ πατέρα ἐπικαλεῖσθαι. πάτερ
ἡμῶν ὁ ἐν τοῖς οὐρανοῖς. οὐρανοὶ δὲ εἶεν ἂν καὶ οἱ τὴν
τοῦ ἐπουρανίου φοροῦντες εἰκόνα, ἐν οἷς ἐστι θεὸς ἐνοικῶν καὶ
ἐμπεριπατῶν.

12. 'Hallowed be Thy Name'

Ἁγιασθήτω τὸ ὄνομά σου. ἅγιόν ἐστι τῇ φύσει τὸ τοῦ
θεοῦ ὄνομα, κἂν λέγωμεν κἂν μὴ λέγωμεν. ἐπεὶ δὲ καὶ ἐν τοῖς
ἁμαρτάνουσιν ἔσθ' ὅτε βεβηλοῦται κατὰ τὸ δι' ὑμᾶς τὸ
ὄνομά μου διὰ παντὸς βλασφημεῖται ἐν τοῖς
ἔθνεσιν, εὐχόμεθα ἐν ἡμῖν ἁγιασθῆναι τὸ ὄνομα τοῦ θεοῦ·
οὐχ ὅτι ἐκ τοῦ μὴ εἶναι ἅγιον ἐπὶ τὸ εἶναι ἔρχεται, ἀλλ' ὅτι
ἐν ἡμῖν ἅγιον γίνεται ἁγιαζομένοις καὶ ἄξια τοῦ ἁγιασμοῦ
ποιοῦσιν.

13. *'Thy Kingdom Come'*

Ἐλθέτω ἡ βασιλεία σου. καθαρᾶς ψυχῆς ἐστι τὸ σὺν
παρρησίᾳ φάναι " ἐλθέτω ἡ βασιλεία σου ". ὁ γὰρ ἀκούσας
Παύλου λέγοντος μὴ οὖν βασιλευέτω ἡ ἁμαρτία ἐν τῷ
θνητῷ ὑμῶν σώματι, ἀλλὰ καθάρας ἑαυτὸν πράξει καὶ
ἐννοίᾳ καὶ λόγῳ ἐρεῖ τῷ θεῷ· ἐλθέτω ἡ βασιλεία σου.

14. *'Thy Will be done, as in Heaven so on Earth'*

Γενηθήτω τὸ θέλημά σου, ὡς ἐν οὐρανῷ, καὶ ἐπὶ
τῆς γῆς. οἱ θεῖοι καὶ μακάριοι τοῦ θεοῦ ἄγγελοι τὸ τοῦ θεοῦ
θέλημα ποιοῦσι, καθὼς Δαβὶδ ψάλλων ἔλεγεν· εὐλογεῖτε
τὸν κύριον πάντες οἱ ἄγγελοι αὐτοῦ, δυνατοὶ ἰσχύι,
ποιοῦντες τὰ θελήματα αὐτοῦ. δυνάμει τοίνυν εὐχόμενος τοῦτο λέγεις· ὡς ἐν ἀγγέλοις γίνεταί σου τὸ θέλημα,
οὕτω καὶ ἐπὶ τῆς γῆς ἐν ἐμοὶ γένοιτο, δέσποτα.

15. *'Give us this day our supersubstantial Bread'*

Τὸν ἄρτον ἡμῶν τὸν ἐπιούσιον δὸς ἡμῖν σήμερον.
ὁ ἄρτος οὗτος ὁ κοινὸς οὐκ ἔστιν ἐπιούσιος· ἄρτος δὲ οὗτος ὁ
ἅγιος ἐπιούσιός ἐστιν, ἀντὶ τοῦ ἐπὶ τὴν οὐσίαν τῆς ψυχῆς
κατατασσόμενος. οὗτος ὁ ἄρτος οὐκ εἰς κοιλίαν χωρεῖ καὶ
εἰς ἀφεδρῶνα ἐκβάλλεται, ἀλλ' εἰς πᾶσάν σου τὴν σύστασιν
ἀναδίδοται εἰς ὠφέλειαν σώματος καὶ ψυχῆς. τὸ δὲ σήμερον
ἀντὶ τοῦ καθ' ἡμέραν λέγει, ὡς καὶ ὁ Παῦλος ἔλεγεν· ἄχρις
οὗ τὸ σήμερον καλεῖται.

16. *'And forgive us our Debts, as we forgive our Debtors'*

Καὶ ἄφες ἡμῖν τὰ ὀφειλήματα ἡμῶν, ὡς καὶ ἡμεῖς
ἀφίεμεν τοῖς ὀφειλέταις ἡμῶν. πολλὰ γὰρ ἔχομεν

ἁμαρτήματα· πταίομεν γὰρ καὶ ἐν λόγῳ καὶ ἐν διανοίᾳ καὶ
πλεῖστα καταγνώσεως ἄξια ποιοῦμεν. καὶ ἐὰν εἴπωμεν,
ὅτι ἁμαρτίαν οὐχ ἔχομεν, ψευδόμεθα, ὡς λέγει Ἰωάν-
νης. καὶ πρὸς τὸν θεὸν τιθέμεθα συνθήκας, συγχωρῆσαι ἡμῖν
παρακαλοῦντες τὰ ἁμαρτήματα, ὡς καὶ ἡμεῖς τοῖς πέλας τὰ
ὀφειλήματα. ἐννοοῦντες τοίνυν, ἀνθ᾽ οἵων οἷα λαμβάνομεν, μὴ
ἀναμείνωμεν μηδὲ ὑπερτιθώμεθα συγχωρεῖν ἀλλήλοις. τὰ
πταίσματα τὰ γινόμενα εἰς ἡμᾶς μικρά ἐστι καὶ εὐτελῆ καὶ
εὐδιάλυτα, τὰ δὲ εἰς θεὸν ὑφ᾽ ἡμῶν γενόμενα μεγάλα ἐστί, τῆς
αὐτοῦ μόνης δεόμενα φιλανθρωπίας. πρόσεχε οὖν, μὴ διὰ τὰ
μικρὰ καὶ εὐτελῆ εἰς σὲ ἁμαρτήματα ἀποκλείσῃς σεαυτῷ τῶν
βαρυτάτων ἁμαρτημάτων τὴν παρὰ θεοῦ συγχώρησιν.

17. 'And lead us not into Temptation'

Καὶ μὴ εἰσενέγκῃς ἡμᾶς εἰς πειρασμόν, κύριε. ἆρα
τοῦτο διδάσκει εὔχεσθαι ἡμᾶς, μηδόλως πειρασθῆναι, ὁ κύριος;
καὶ πῶς εἴρηται ἀλλαχοῦ· ἀνὴρ ἀπείραστος ἀδόκιμος,
καὶ πάλιν· πᾶσαν χαρὰν ἡγήσασθε, ἀδελφοί μου, ὅταν
πειρασμοῖς περιπέσητε ποικίλοις; ἀλλὰ μήποτε τὸ
εἰσελθεῖν ἐστιν εἰς πειρασμὸν τὸ καταβαπτισθῆναι ὑπὸ τοῦ
πειρασμοῦ· ἔοικε γὰρ ὁ πειρασμὸς ὥσπερ χειμάρρῳ τινὶ
δυσκόλῳ πρὸς διάβασιν. οἱ μὲν οὖν ἐν πειρασμοῖς μὴ κατα-
βαπτιζόμενοι διαβαίνουσιν, ἄριστοί τινες κολυμβηταὶ γινόμενοι καὶ μηδόλως ὑπ᾽ αὐτῶν κατασυρόμενοι. οἱ δὲ μὴ
τοιοῦτοι εἰσιόντες καταβαπτίζονται· οἷον ὡς ἐπὶ παραδεί-
γματος Ἰούδας εἰσελθὼν εἰς τὸν τῆς φιλοχρηματίας πειρασμὸν
οὐ διενήξατο, ἀλλὰ καταβαπτισθεὶς καὶ σωματικῶς καὶ
πνευματικῶς ἀπεπνίγη. Πέτρος εἰσῆλθεν εἰς τὸν τῆς ἀρνή-
σεως πειρασμόν, ἀλλὰ εἰσελθὼν οὐκ ἐβαπτίσθη, ἀλλὰ γεν-
ναίως διανηξάμενος ἐρρύσθη ἀπὸ τοῦ πειρασμοῦ.

Ἄκουε πάλιν ἀλλαχοῦ ὁλοκλήρων ἁγίων χοροῦ εὐχαριστοῦν
τος ἐπὶ τῷ ἐξαιρεθῆναι τοῦ πειρασμοῦ· ἐδοκίμασας ἡμᾶς
ὁ θεός, ἐπύρωσας ἡμᾶς ὡς πυροῦται τὸ ἀργύριον·
εἰσήγαγες ἡμᾶς εἰς τὴν παγίδα, ἔθου θλίψεις ἐπὶ
τὸν νῶτον ἡμῶν, ἐπεβίβασας ἀνθρώπους ἐπὶ τὰς
κεφαλὰς ἡμῶν. διήλθομεν διὰ πυρὸς καὶ ὕδατος,
καὶ ἐξήγαγες ἡμᾶς εἰς ἀναψυχήν. ὁρᾷς αὐτοὺς παρρη
σιαζομένους ἐπὶ τῷ διελθεῖν καὶ μὴ ἐμπαγῆναι. καὶ ἐξήγαγες
ἡμᾶς, φησίν, εἰς ἀναψυχήν· τὸ εἰς ἀναψυχὴν ἐλθεῖν αὐτούς
ἐστι τὸ ἀπὸ πειρασμοῦ ῥυσθῆναι.

18. 'But deliver us from Evil'

Ἀλλὰ ῥῦσαι ἡμᾶς ἀπὸ τοῦ πονηροῦ. εἰ ἦν τὸ " μὴ εἰσ
ενέγκῃς ἡμᾶς εἰς πειρασμὸν " τὸ τοῦ μηδόλως πειρασθῆναι
παραστατικόν, οὐκ ἂν ἔλεγεν " ἀλλὰ ῥῦσαι ἡμᾶς ἀπὸ τοῦ
πονηροῦ ". πονηρὸς δὲ ὁ ἀντικείμενος δαίμων, ἀφ' οὗ ῥυ
σθῆναι εὐχόμεθα.

Εἶτα μετὰ πλήρωσιν τῆς εὐχῆς λέγεις ἀμήν, ἐπισφραγίζων
διὰ τοῦ ἀμήν, ὃ σημαίνει " γένοιτο ", τὰ ἐν τῇ θεοδιδάκτῳ
εὐχῇ.

19. 'Holy Things to Holy People'

Μετὰ ταῦτα λέγει ὁ ἱερεύς· "τὰ ἅγια τοῖς ἁγίοις". ἅγια τὰ
προκείμενα, ἐπιφοίτησιν δεξάμενα ἁγίου πνεύματος· ἅγιοι καὶ
ὑμεῖς, πνεύματος ἁγίου καταξιωθέντες. τὰ ἅγια οὖν τοῖς
ἁγίοις κατάλληλα. εἶτα ὑμεῖς λέγετε· "εἷς ἅγιος, εἷς κύριος,
Ἰησοῦς Χριστός". ἀληθῶς γὰρ εἷς ἅγιος, φύσει ἅγιος· ἡμεῖς
δὲ καὶ ἅγιοι, ἀλλ' οὐ φύσει, ἀλλὰ μετοχῇ καὶ ἀσκήσει καὶ
εὐχῇ.

20. The Communion Melody

Μετὰ ταῦτα ἀκούετε τοῦ ψάλλοντος μετὰ μέλους θείου προτρεπομένου ὑμᾶς εἰς τὴν κοινωνίαν τῶν ἁγίων μυστηρίων καὶ λέγοντος· γεύσασθε καὶ ἴδετε, ὅτι χρηστὸς ὁ κύριος. μὴ τῷ λάρυγγι τῷ σωματικῷ ἐπιτρέπητε τὸ κριτικόν, οὐχί, ἀλλὰ τῇ ἀνενδοιάστῳ πίστει· γευόμενοι γὰρ οὐκ ἄρτου καὶ οἴνου κελεύονται γεύσασθαι, ἀλλὰ ἀντιτύπου σώματος καὶ αἵματος τοῦ Χριστοῦ.

21. How to receive the Body of Christ

Προσιὼν οὖν μὴ τεταμένοις τοῖς τῶν χειρῶν καρποῖς προσέρχου μηδὲ διηρημένοις τοῖς δακτύλοις· ἀλλὰ τὴν ἀριστερὰν θρόνον ποιήσας τῇ δεξιᾷ, ὡς μελλούσῃ βασιλέα ὑποδέχεσθαι, καὶ κοιλάνας τὴν παλάμην δέχου τὸ σῶμα τοῦ Χριστοῦ, ἐπιλέγων τὸ ἀμήν. μετ᾽ ἀσφαλείας οὖν ἁγιάσας τοὺς ὀφθαλμοὺς τῇ ἐπαφῇ τοῦ ἁγίου σώματος μεταλάμβανε, προσέχων, μὴ παραπολέσῃς τι ἐκ τούτου αὐτοῦ· ὅπερ γὰρ ἐὰν ἀπολέσῃς, τούτῳ ὡς ἀπὸ οἰκείου δηλονότι ἐζημιώθης μέλους. εἰπὲ γάρ μοι, εἴ τίς σοι ἔδωκε ψήγματα χρυσίου, οὐκ ἂν μετὰ πάσης ἀσφαλείας ἐκράτεις, φυλαττόμενος, μή τι αὐτῶν παραπολέσῃς καὶ ζημίαν ὑποστῇς; οὐ πολλῷ οὖν μᾶλλον ἀσφαλέστερον τοῦ χρυσίου καὶ λίθων τιμίων τιμιωτέρου διασκοπήσεις ὑπὲρ τοῦ μὴ ψίχαν σοι ἐκπεσεῖν;

22. How to receive His Blood

Εἶτα μετὰ τὸ κοινωνῆσαί σε τοῦ σώματος Χριστοῦ προσέρχου καὶ τῷ ποτηρίῳ τοῦ αἵματος, μὴ ἀνατείνων τὰς χεῖρας, ἀλλὰ κύπτων καὶ τρόπῳ προσκυνήσεως καὶ σεβάσματος λέγων τὸ ἀμὴν ἁγιάζου καὶ ἐκ τοῦ αἵματος μεταλαμ-

βάνων Χριστοῦ. ἔτι δὲ τῆς νοτίδος ἐνούσης τοῖς χείλεσί σου
χερσὶν ἐπαφώμενος καὶ ὀφθαλμοὺς καὶ μέτωπον καὶ τὰ λοιπὰ
ἁγίαζε αἰσθητήρια. εἶτα ἀναμείνας τὴν εὐχὴν εὐχαρίστει τῷ
θεῷ τῷ καταξιώσαντί σε τῶν τηλικούτων μυστηρίων.

23. Benediction

Κατέχετε ταύτας τὰς παραδόσεις ἀσπίλους καὶ ἀπροσκόπους
ἑαυτοὺς διαφυλάξατε. τῆς κοινωνίας ἑαυτοὺς μὴ ἀπορρήξητε,
μὴ διὰ μολυσμὸν ἁμαρτιῶν τῶν ἱερῶν τούτων καὶ πνευματικῶν
ἑαυτοὺς ἀποστερήσητε μυστηρίων.

Ὁ δὲ θεὸς τῆς εἰρήνης ἁγιάσαι ὑμᾶς ὁλοτελεῖς,
καὶ ὁλόκληρον ὑμῶν τὸ σῶμα καὶ ἡ ψυχὴ καὶ τὸ
πνεῦμα ἐν τῇ παρουσίᾳ τοῦ κυρίου ἡμῶν Ἰησοῦ
Χριστοῦ διατηρηθείη. ᾧ ἡ δόξα, τιμὴ καὶ κράτος σὺν
πατρὶ [καὶ υἱῷ] καὶ ἁγίῳ πνεύματι νῦν καὶ ἀεὶ καὶ εἰς τοὺς
αἰῶνας τῶν αἰώνων. ἀμήν.

THE PROCATECHESIS

1. ALREADY is there on you the savour of blessedness, O ye who are soon to be enlightened: already are you gathering spiritual flowers, to weave heavenly crowns withal: already hath the fragrance of the Holy Ghost refreshed you: already are you at the entrance-hall of the King's house: may you be brought into it by the King! For now the blossoms of the trees have budded; may but the fruit likewise be perfected! Thus far, your names have been given in, and the roll-call made for service; there are the torches of the bridal train, and the longings after heavenly citizenship, and a good purpose, and a hope attendant; for he cannot lie who hath said, *To them that love God, all things work together for good.*[1] God is indeed lavish in His benefits: yet He looks for each man's honest resolve: so the Apostle subjoins, *To those who are called according to their purpose.* Honesty of purpose makes thee *called*: for though the body be here, yet if the mind be away, it avails nothing.

2. Even Simon Magus once came to the Laver of Baptism,[2] he was baptized, but not enlightened. His body he dipped in water, but admitted not the Spirit

---

[1] Rom. 8. 28.   [2] Acts 8. 13.

to illuminate his heart. His body went down and came up; but his soul was not buried together with Christ, nor with Him raised. I mention such instances of falls, that thou mayest not fail; *for these things happéned to them for ensamples, and they are written for the admonition*[1] of those, who up to this day are ever coming. Let no one of you be found tempting grace: let no *root of bitterness spring up, and trouble you*:[2] let not any of you enter, saying, Come, let us see what the faithful do: I will go in and see, that I may learn what is done. Expectest thou to see, and not to be seen: and thinkest thou to busy thee with what is doing, and God not be busy with thine heart the while?

3. A certain man in the Gospels[3] busily pried into the marriage feast: he took an unbecoming garment, came in, sat down, and ate; for the bridegroom permitted thus far: whereas, when he saw the white robes of all, he ought himself likewise to have taken such another; yet he shared like meats with them, being unlike them in fashion and in purpose. But the bridegroom, though bountiful, was not undiscerning; and, as he went round to each of the guests and viewed them, (not that he was careful how they feasted, but how they behaved,) seeing a stranger, not having a wedding-garment on, he said to him, *Friend, how camest thou in hither?* With what stained raiments? with what a conscience? What, though the porter stopped thee not, because of the bountifulness of the entertainer? what, though thou wert ignorant in what fashion thou shouldest enter into

[1] 1 Cor. 10. 11.   [2] Heb. 12. 15.   [3] Mat. 22. 12.

the banquet? yet thou camest in, thou didst see the glistering fashion of the guests. Shouldest thou not have learned at least from what thou sawest? Shouldest thou not have made a seasonable retreat, that thou mightest have a seasonable return? but now hast thou turned in unseasonably, that unseasonably thou mightest be thrust out. So he commands his servants, Bind his feet, which have daringly intruded,—bind his hands, which were not skilled to robe him in the bright garment; and cast him into the outer darkness; for he is unworthy of the wedding torches. Thou hast seen how he fared then; take heed to thyself.

4. For we, the ministers of Christ, have admitted every man, and holding as it were the place of doorkeepers, have left the door unfastened. Thou hast been free then to enter with a soul bemired with sins, and a defiled purpose. Entered thou hast: thou hast passed, thou hast been enrolled. Seest thou these venerable arrangements of the Church? Viewest thou her order and discipline, the reading of the Scriptures, the presence of the religious, the course of teaching? Let then the place affect thee, let the sight sober thee. Depart in good time now, and enter tomorrow in better. If avarice has been the fashion of thy soul, put on another, and then come in: put off what thou hadst, cloke it not over: put off, I pray thee, fornication and uncleanness, and put on the most bright robe of soberness. This charge I give thee, before Jesus the spouse of souls come in, and see their fashion. Thou art allowed a distant day; thou hast a penitence of forty; thou hast

full time to put off, and to wash thee, to put on, and to enter in. But if thou abide in thy evil purpose, he who speaks is blameless, but thou must not look for grace: for though the water shall receive thee, the Spirit will not accept thee. Whoso is conscious of a wound, let him take the salve: whoso has fallen, let him rise: let there be no Simon among you, no hypocrisy, no idle curiosity about the matter.

5. Perhaps thou comest on another ground. A man may be wishing to pay court to a woman, and on that account come hither: and the same applies to women likewise: again, a slave often wishes thus to please his master, or one friend another. I avail myself of this angler's bait, and receive thee, as one who has come indeed with an unsound purpose, but art to be saved by a good hope. Thou knewest not perchance whither thou wast coming, nor what net was taking thee. Thou art within the Church's nets, submit to be taken; flee not, for Jesus would secure thee, not to make thee die, but by death to make thee live. For thou must die and rise again; thou hast heard the Apostle saying, *Dead indeed to sin, but alive unto righteousness.*[1] Die then to thy sins, and live to righteousness: yea, from this day forth, live.

6. Look, I beseech thee, how great dignity Jesus presents to thee. Thou wert called a Catechumen, which means, hearing with the ears, hearing hope, and not perceiving; hearing mysteries, yet not understanding: hearing Scriptures, yet not knowing their depth. Thou

[1] Rom. 6. 11.

no longer hearest with the ears, but thou hearest within; for the indwelling Spirit henceforth fashions thy mind into a house of God. When thou shalt hear what is written concerning mysteries, then thou shalt understand, what hitherto thou knewest not. And think not it is a trifle thou receivest. Thou, a wretched man, receivest the Name of God; for hear the words of Paul, *God is faithful*;[1] and another Scripture, *God is faithful and just*.[2] This the Psalmist foreseeing, since men were to receive the Name ascribed to God, said in the person of God, *I have said, ye are Gods, and are all the children of the Most High*.[3] But beware lest with the name of believer thou have the purpose of an unbeliever. Thou hast entered into the struggle; labour therefore in the race, for season thou hast none other such. If thou hadst thy wedding day before thee, wouldest thou not make light of aught besides, and be full of preparations for the feast? And wilt thou not then, when on the eve of consecrating thy soul to a heavenly spouse, let go carnal things that thou mayest take hold of spiritual?

7. The bath of Baptism we may not receive twice or thrice; else, it might be said, Though I fail once, I shall go right next time: whereas if thou failest once, there is no setting things right, for there is *One Lord, and one Faith, and One Baptism*: none but heretics are rebaptized, since their former baptism was not baptism.

8. For God seeks nothing else from us, save a good purpose. Say not, How are my sins blotted out? I tell thee, from willing, from believing; what is shorter than

[1] 1 Cor. 1. 9.   [2] 1 John 1. 9.   [3] Ps. 82. 6.

this? But if thy lips declare thy willing, but thy heart is silent, He knows the heart who judgeth thee. Cease then henceforth from every wicked thing: refrain thy tongue from light words, thine eye from sin, thy mind from roving after useless matters.

9. Let thy feet hasten to the Catechizings, receive with earnestness the Exorcisms; for whether thou art breathed upon, or exorcized, the Ordinance is to thee salvation. It is as though thou hadst gold unwrought or alloyed, blended with various substances, with brass, and tin, and iron, and lead: we seek to have the gold pure, but it cannot be cleansed from foreign substances without fire. Even so, without Exorcisms, the soul cannot be cleansed; and they are divine, collected from the divine Scriptures. Thy face is veiled, that thy mind may be henceforth at leisure; lest a roving eye cause a roving heart. But though thine eyes be veiled, thine ears are not hindered receiving what is saving. For as the goldsmith, conveying the blast upon the fire through delicate instruments, and as it were breathing on the gold which is hid in the hollow of the forge, stimulates the flame it acts upon, and so obtains what he is seeking; so also, exorcizers, infusing fear by the Holy Ghost, and setting the soul on fire in the crucible of the body, make the evil spirit flee, who is our enemy, and salvation and the hope of eternal life abide; and henceforth the soul, cleansed from its sins, hath salvation. Let us then, brethren, abide in hope, surrendering ourselves and hoping; so may the God of all, seeing our purpose, cleanse us from sins, and impart to us good

hopes of our estate, and grant us saving penitence! He who calls, is God, and thou art the person called.

10. Abide thou in the Catechizings: though our discourse be long, let not thy mind be wearied out. For thou art receiving thine armour against the antagonist power; against heresies, against Jews, and Samaritans, and Gentiles. Thou hast many enemies; take to thee many darts; thou hast many to hurl them at. And thou hast need to learn how to hurl them at the Greek; how to do battle against heretic, against Jew and Samaritan. The armour indeed is ready, and most ready is the sword of the Spirit; but thou also must stretch forth thy hands with good resolve, that thou mayest war the Lord's warfare, mayest overcome the powers that oppose thee, mayest escape defeat from every heretical attempt.

11. This charge also I give thee. Study the things that are spoken, and keep them for ever. Think not that they are the ordinary Homilies, which are excellent indeed, and trustworthy, but if neglected today, may be attended to tomorrow. On the contrary, the teaching concerning the laver of regeneration, delivered in course, how shall it be made up, if today it be neglected? Consider it to be the planting season; unless we dig, and that deeply, how shall that afterwards be planted rightly, which has once been planted ill? Or consider Catechizing to be a kind of building: unless we dig deep, and lay the foundation,—unless by successive fastenings in the masonry, we bind the frame-work of the house together, that no opening be detected, nor the

work be left unsound, naught avails all our former labour. But stone must succeed stone in course, and corner must follow corner, and, inequalities being smoothed away, the masonry must rise regular. In like manner we are bringing to thee the stones, as it were, of knowledge; thou must hear concerning the Living God; concerning Judgement; concerning Christ; concerning the Resurrection; and many things are made to follow one the other, which though now dropped one by one, at length are presented in harmonious connexion. But if thou wilt not connect them into one whole, and remember what is first, and what is second, the builder indeed buildeth, but the building will be unstable.

12. Now when the Catechizing has taken place, should a Catechumen ask what the teachers have said, tell nothing to a stranger; for we deliver to thee a mystery, even the hope of the life to come: keep the mystery for Him who pays thee. Let no man say to thee, What harm, if I also know it? So the sick ask for wine; but if it be unseasonably given them, it occasions delirium, and two evils follow; the sick man dies, and the physician gets an ill name. Thus is it with the Catechumen also if he should hear from the Believer: the Catechumen is made delirious, for not understanding what he has heard, he finds fault with it, and scoffs at it, and the Believer bears the blame of a betrayer. But now thou art standing on the frontiers; see thou let out nothing; not that the things spoken do not deserve telling, but the ear that hears does not deserve receiving. Thou thyself wast once a Catechumen, and

then I told thee not what was coming. When thou hast by practice reached the height of what is taught thee, then wilt thou understand that the Catechumens are unworthy to hear them.

13. Ye who have been enrolled, are become the sons and daughters of one Mother. When ye have entered in before the hour of exorcizing, let one of you speak what may promote godliness: and if any of your number be not present, seek for him. If thou wert called to a banquet, wouldest thou not wait for thy fellow-guest? If thou hadst a brother, wouldest thou not seek thy brother's good? Henceforth meddle not unprofit-ably with external matters; what the city hath done, or the town, or Prince, or Bishop, or Presbyter. Look upward, thy present hour hath need of that. *Be still and know that I am God.*[1] If thou seest the Believers ministering without care, yet they enjoy security, they know what they have received, they are in possession of grace. But thou art just now in the turn of the scale, to be received or not: thou must not copy those who are free from care, but cherish fear.

14. And when the Exorcism is made, until the rest who are exorcized be come, let the men stay with the men, and the women with the women. Here I would allude to Noah's ark; in which were Noah and his sons, and his wife and their wives; and though the ark was one, and the door was shut, yet had things been ar-ranged suitably. And though the Church be shut, and all of you within it, yet let there be a distinction, of men

[1] Ps. 46. 10.

with men and women with women. Let not the ground
of your salvation become a means of destruction. Even
though there be good ground for your sitting near each
other, yet let passions be away. Then, let the men
when sitting have a useful book; and let one read, and
another listen: and if there be no book, let the one pray,
and another speak something useful; and let the party
of young women be so ordered, that they may either
be singing or reading, but without noise, so that their
lips may speak, but others may not hear. *For*, says the
Apostle, *I suffer not a woman to speak in the Church*:[1]
and let the married woman do the same; let her pray,
moving her lips, her voice not sounding: that Samuel
may come, and thy barren soul may bear *the salvation
of God who hears prayer*;[2] for this is the meaning of the
word Samuel.

15. I will behold each man's earnestness; each
woman's reverence. Let your mind be refined as by
fire unto reverence, let your soul be forged as metal.
Let the stubbornness of unbelief feel the anvil, let the
superfluous scales drop off as of iron, and what is pure
remain: let the rust be rubbed off, and the true metal
be left. May God at length show you that night, that
darkness which shows like day, concerning which it is
said, *The darkness shall not be darkened from thee, and
the night shall be light as the day*.[3] At that time to each
man and woman among you may the gate of paradise
be opened; may you then enjoy the fragrant waters,
which contain Christ; may you then receive Christ's

[1] 1 Cor. 14. 34.   [2] Cf. 1 Sam. 1. 13, 17.   [3] Ps. 139. 12. LXX.

name, and the efficacious power of divine things! Even
now, I beseech you, lift up the eye of your understanding; imagine the angelic choirs, and God the Lord of
all sitting, and His Only-Begotten Son sitting with
Him on His right hand, and the Spirit with them present, and thrones and dominions doing service, and
each man and woman among you receiving salvation.
Even now let your ears ring with the sound: long for
that glorious sound, which after your salvation, the
angels shall chant over you, *Blessed are they whose
iniquities have been forgiven, and whose sins have been
covered*;[1] when, like stars of the Church, you shall enter
in it, bright in the outward man and radiant in your
souls.

16. Great indeed is the Baptism which is offered you.
It is a ransom to captives; the remission of offences; the
death of sin; the regeneration of the soul; the garment
of light; the holy seal indissoluble; the chariot to
heaven; the luxury of paradise; a procuring of the
kingdom; the gift of adoption. But a serpent by the
wayside is watching the passengers; beware lest he bite
thee with unbelief; he sees so many receiving salvation,
and seeks to devour some of them. Thou art going to
the Father of Spirits, but thou art going past that serpent; how then must thou pass him? Have *thy feet
shod with the preparation of the gospel of peace*;[2] that even
if he bite, he may not hurt thee. Have faith indwelling,
strong hope, a sandal of power, wherewith to pass the
enemy, and enter the presence of thy Lord. Prepare

[1] Ps. 32. 1.　　　　　[2] Eph. 6. 15.

thine own heart to receive doctrine, to have fellowship in holy mysteries. Pray more often, that God may make thee worthy of the heavenly and immortal mysteries. Let neither day be without its work, nor night, but when sleep fails thine eyes, at once abandon thy thoughts to prayer. And shouldest thou find any shameful, any base imagination rising, reflect upon God's judgement, to remind thee of salvation; give up thy mind to sacred studies, that it may forget wicked things. If thou find anyone saying to thee, And art thou going to the water, to be baptized in it? what, hath not the city baths of late? Be sure that it is the dragon of the sea, who is plotting this against thee; give no heed to the lips of him who speaketh, but to God who worketh. Guard thine own soul, that thou mayest escape the snare, that abiding in hope, thou mayest become the heir of everlasting salvation.

17. We indeed, as men, charge and teach these things; for you, see you make not our building *hay and stubble, and chaff*; that we may not *suffer loss, our work being burnt*; but make our work, *gold and silver and precious stones*.[1] It is for me to speak, but thine to second me, and God's part to perfect. Let us nerve our minds; let us brace up our souls; let us prepare our hearts; the race is for our soul, our hope about eternal things. God is able, who knows your hearts, and perceives who is sincere, and who is a hypocrite, both to preserve the sincere and to give faith to the hypocrite; nay even to the unbeliever, if he give Him but his

[1] 1 Cor. 3. 12, 15.

heart. And may He *blot out the handwriting that is against you*,[1] and grant you forgiveness of your former trespasses; may He plant you in the Church, and enlist you for Himself, putting on you the armour of righteousness! And may He fill you with the heavenly things of the New Testament, and give you the indelible seal of the Holy Spirit, throughout all ages, in Christ Jesus our Lord, to whom be glory for ever and ever! Amen.

[1] Col. 2. 14.

MYSTAGOGICAL CATECHESIS I

ON THE RITES BEFORE BAPTISM

1 Peter 5. 8–14

Be sober, be vigilant; because your adversary the devil, as a roaring lion, walketh about, seeking whom he may devour, &c.

1. I LONG ago desired, true-born and dearly beloved children of the Church, to discourse to you concerning these spiritual and heavenly Mysteries; but knowing well, that seeing is far more persuasive than hearing, I waited till this season; that finding you more open to the influence of my words from this your experience, I might take and lead you to the brighter and more fragrant meadow of this present paradise; especially as ye have been made fit to receive the more sacred Mysteries, having been counted worthy of divine and life-giving Baptism. It remaining therefore to dress for you a board of more perfect instruction, let us now teach you exactly about these things, that ye may know the deep meaning to you-ward of what was done on that evening of your baptism.

2. First, ye entered into the outer hall of the Baptistery, and there facing towards the West, ye heard the command to stretch forth your hand, and as in the presence of Satan ye renounced him. Now ye must know that this figure is found in ancient history. For when Pharaoh, that most cruel and ruthless tyrant,

oppressed the free and high-born people of the Hebrews, God sent Moses to bring them out of the evil thraldom of the Egyptians. Then the door-posts were anointed with the blood of the lamb, that the destroyer might flee from the houses which had the sign of the blood; and the Hebrew people was marvellously delivered. The enemy, however, after their rescue, pursued them, and saw the sea wondrously parted for them; nevertheless he went on, following in their footsteps, and was all at once overwhelmed and engulfed in the Red Sea.

3. Now turn from the ancient to the recent, from the figure to the reality. There we have Moses sent from God to Egypt; here, Christ, sent by His Father into the world: there, that Moses might lead forth an oppressed people out of Egypt; here, that Christ might rescue mankind who are whelmed under sins: there, the blood of a lamb was the spell against the destroyer; here, the blood of the unblemished Lamb Jesus Christ is made the charm to scare evil spirits: there, the tyrant pursued even to the sea that ancient people; and in like manner this daring and shameless spirit, the author of evil, followed thee, even to the very streams of salvation. The tyrant of old was drowned in the sea; and this present one disappears in the salutary water.

4. However, thou art bidden with arm outstretched to say to him as though actually present, I RENOUNCE THEE, SATAN. I wish to say, wherefore ye stand facing to the West; for it is necessary. Since the West is the region of sensible darkness, and he being darkness, has

his dominion also in darkness, ye therefore, looking with a symbolical meaning towards the West, renounce that dark and gloomy potentate. What then did each of you standing up say? 'I renounce thee, Satan, thou wicked and most cruel tyrant!' meaning, 'I fear thy might no longer; for Christ hath overthrown it, having partaken with me of flesh and blood, that through these He *might by death destroy death*, that I might not for ever be *subject to bondage*.[1] I renounce thee, thou crafty and most subtle serpent. I renounce thee, plotter as thou art, who under the guise of friendship didst work all disobedience, and bring about the apostasy of our first parents. I renounce thee, Satan, the artificer and abettor of all wickedness.'

5. Then in the second sentence thou art told to say, AND ALL THY WORKS. Now the works of Satan are all sin, which it is necessary to renounce also;—just as if a man has escaped a tyrant, he would have doubtless escaped his instruments also. All sin therefore, according to its kinds, is included in the works of the devil. Only know this; that all that thou sayest, especially at that most thrilling hour, is written in God's books; when therefore thou doest any thing contrary to these, thou shalt be judged as *a transgressor*.[2] Thou renouncest therefore the works of Satan; I mean, all deeds and thoughts which are against thy better judgement.

6. Then thou sayest, AND ALL HIS POMP. Now the pomp of the devil is the madness of shows, and horse-races, and hunting, and all such vanity: from which

[1] Heb. 2. 14, 15.   [2] Gal. 2. 18.

that holy man praying to be delivered, says unto God, *Turn away mine eyes from beholding vanity.*[1] Be not interested in the madness of the shows, where thou wilt behold the wanton gestures of players, carried on with mockeries and all unseemliness, and the frantic dancing of effeminate men;—nor in the madness of them who in hunts expose themselves to wild beasts, that they may pamper their miserable appetite; who, that they may indulge their belly with meats, become themselves truly meat for the belly of ravenous beasts; and to speak justly, they for the sake of their proper god, their belly, cast away their life headlong in single combats. Shun also horse-races, that frantic spectacle, which subverts souls. For all these are the pomp of the devil.

7. Moreover, things also hung up at idol festivals, either meat or bread, or other such things which are polluted by the invocation of the unclean spirits, are reckoned in the pomp of the devil. For as the Bread and Wine of the Eucharist before the holy invocation of the Adorable Trinity was simple bread and wine, while after the invocation the Bread becomes the Body of Christ, and the Wine the Blood of Christ, so in like manner, such meats belonging to the pomp of Satan, though in their own nature plain and simple, become profane by the invocation of the evil spirit.

8. And after this thou sayest, AND ALL THY SERVICE. Now the service of the devil is prayer in idol temples; things done to the honour of lifeless idols; the lighting of lamps, or burning of incense by fountains or rivers,

[1] Ps. 119. 37.

(for some cheated by dreams or by evil spirits, have passed to these places, thinking to find a cure even for their bodily ailments,) and the like. Go not therefore after them. The watching of birds, divination, omens, or amulets, or charms written on leaves, sorceries, or other evil arts, and all such things, are services to the devil; therefore shun them. For if after renouncing Satan and ranging thyself with Christ, thou fall under their influence, thou shalt find the tyrant more bitter in his temptations; perchance, because he treated thee of old as his own, and has let thee off from severe slavery, and has been greatly exasperated against thee; so thou wilt be bereaved of Christ, and be tempted by him. Hast thou not heard the old history which tells us of Lot and his daughters? Was not he himself saved with his daughters, because he gained the mountain, while his wife became a pillar of salt, set up as a beacon for ever, as the memorial of her depraved will and her turning back. Take heed therefore to thyself, and turn not again to *what is behind*,[1] going back after having put thine hand to the plough, to the salt savour of this life's doings; but escape to the mountain, to Jesus Christ, that stone hewn without hands, which has filled the world.

9. When therefore thou renouncest Satan, utterly breaking all covenant with him, that ancient league with hell, there is opened to thee the paradise of God, which He planted towards the east, whence for his transgression our first father was exiled; and symbolical

[1] Phil. 3. 13.

of this was thy turning from the west to the east, the place of light. Then thou wert told to say, I believe in the Father, and in the Son, and in the Holy Ghost, and in one Baptism of repentance. Of which things we spoke at length in the former Lectures, as God's grace allowed us.

10. Therefore, guarded by these considerations, be sober. *For* our *adversary the devil*, as was just now read, *as a roaring lion, walketh about, seeking whom he may devour.*[1] In former times death was mighty and devoured; but at the holy Laver of regeneration, God has *wiped away every tear from off all faces.*[2] For thou shalt no more mourn, now that thou hast put off the old man; but thou shalt keep holy-day, clothed in the garment of salvation, even Jesus Christ.

11. And these things were done in the outer chamber. But if God will, when in the succeeding expositions of the Mysteries we have entered into the Holy of Holies, we shall then know the symbolical meaning of what is there accomplished. Now to God the Father, with the Son and the Holy Ghost, be glory, and power, and majesty, for ever and ever. Amen.

[1] 1 Pet. 5. 8.   [2] Is. 25. 8; Rev. 7. 17.

MYSTAGOGICAL CATECHESIS II

ON THE RITES OF BAPTISM

Romans 6. 3–14

Know ye not, that so many of us as were baptized into Jesus Christ, were baptized into His death? &c. . . . for ye are not under the Law, but under grace.

1. THESE introductions into the Mysteries day by day, and these new instructions, which are the announcements of new truths, are profitable to us; and most of all to you, who have been renewed from oldness to newness. Therefore, as is necessary, I will lay before you the sequel of yesterday's Lecture, that ye may learn of what those things, which were done by you in the inner chamber, were the emblems.

2. As soon, therefore, as ye entered in, ye put off your garment; and this was an image of *putting off the old man with his deeds.*[1] Having stripped yourselves, ye were naked; in this also imitating Christ, who hung naked on the Cross, and by His nakedness *spoiled principalities and powers, and openly triumphed over them on the tree.*[2] For since the powers of the enemy made their lair in your members, ye may no longer wear that old vestment; I do not at all mean this visible one, but that *old man, which is corrupt according to the deceitful lusts.*[3] May no soul which has once put him off, again put him on, but say with the Spouse

---

[1] Col. 3. 9. [2] Col. 2. 15. [3] Eph. 4. 22.

of Christ in the Song of Songs, *I have put off my coat,
how shall I put it on ?*[1] O wondrous thing! ye were naked
in the sight of all, and were not ashamed; for truly
ye bore the likeness of the first-formed Adam, who was
naked in the garden, and was not ashamed.

3. Then, when ye were stripped, ye were anointed
with exorcized oil, from the very hairs of your head, to
your feet, and were made partakers of the good olive-
tree, Jesus Christ. For ye were cut off from the
wild olive-tree, and grafted into the good one, and
were made to share the fatness of the true olive-tree.
The exorcized oil therefore was a symbol of the participation of the fatness of Christ, the charm to drive
away every trace of hostile influence. For as the
breathing of the saints, and the invocation of the Name
of God, like fiercest flame, scorch and drive out evil
spirits, so also this exorcized oil receives such virtue
by the invocation of God and by prayer, as not only
to burn and cleanse away the traces of sins, but also
to chase away all the invisible powers of the evil one.

4. After these things, ye were led to the holy pool of
Divine Baptism, as Christ was carried from the Cross
to the Sepulchre which is before our eyes. And each
of you was asked, whether he believed in the name of
the Father, and of the Son, and of the Holy Ghost, and
ye made that saving confession, and descended three
times into the water, and ascended again; here also
covertly pointing by a figure at the three-days burial
of Christ. For as our Saviour passed three days and

[1] Cant. 5. 3.

three nights in the heart of the earth, so you also in your first ascent out of the water, represented the first day of Christ in the earth, and by your descent, the night; for as he who is in the night, sees no more, but he who is in the day, remains in the light, so in descending, ye saw nothing as in the night, but in ascending again, ye were as in the day. And at the self-same moment, ye died and were born; and that Water of salvation was at once your grave and your mother. And what Solomon spoke of others will suit you also; for he said, *There is a time to bear and a time to die*;[1] but to you, on the contrary, the time to die is also the time to be born; and one and the same season brings about both of these, and your birth went hand in hand with your death.

5. O strange and inconceivable thing! we did not really die, we were not really buried, we were not really crucified and raised again, but our imitation was but in a figure, while our salvation is in reality. Christ was actually crucified, and actually buried, and truly rose again; and all these things have been vouchsafed to us, that we, by imitation communicating in His sufferings, might gain salvation in reality. O surpassing loving-kindness! Christ received the nails in His undefiled hands and feet, and endured anguish; while to me without suffering or toil, by the fellowship of His pain He vouchsafes salvation.

6. Let no one then suppose that Baptism is merely the grace of remission of sins, or further, that of

[1] Eccles. 3. 2.

adoption; as John's baptism bestowed only the remission of sins. Nay we know full well, that as it purges our sins, and conveys to us the gift of the Holy Ghost, so also it is the counterpart of Christ's sufferings. For, for this cause Paul, just now read, cried aloud and says, *Know ye not that as many of us as were baptized into Christ Jesus, were baptized into His death? Therefore we are buried with Him by baptism into death.*[1] These words he spake to them who had settled with themselves that Baptism ministers to us the remission of sins, and adoption, but not that further it has communion also in representation with Christ's true sufferings.

7. In order therefore that we may learn, that whatsoever things Christ endured, He suffered them for us and our salvation, and that, in reality and not in appearance, we also are made partakers of His sufferings. Paul cried with all exactness of truth, *For if we have been planted together in the likeness of His death, we shall be also in the likeness of His resurrection.*[2] Well has he said, *planted together*. For since the true Vine was planted in this place, we also by partaking in the Baptism of death, *have been planted together with Him*. And fix thy mind with much attention on the words of the Apostle. He has not said, 'For if we have been planted together in His death', but, *in the likeness of His death*. For upon Christ death came in reality, for His soul was truly separated from His body, and His burial was true, for His holy body was wrapt in pure linen; and every thing happened to Him truly; but in

[1] Rom. 6. 3.   [2] Ibid. 5.

your case only the likeness of death and sufferings, whereas of salvation, not the likeness, but the reality.

8. Of these things then having been sufficiently instructed, keep them, I beseech you, in your remembrance; that I also, unworthy though I be, may say of you, *Now I love you, brethren, because ye remember me in all things, and keep the ordinances, as I delivered them unto you.*[1] And God, who has presented you as it were alive from the dead, is able to grant unto you to walk in newness of life; because His is the glory and the power, now and for ever. Amen.

MYSTAGOGICAL CATECHESIS III

ON THE HOLY CHRISM

1 John 2. 20–8

But ye have an unction from the Holy One, &c. . . . that, when He shall appear, we may have confidence, and not be ashamed before Him at His coming.

1. HAVING been *baptized into Christ,* and *put on Christ,*[2] ye have been made conformable to the Son of God; for God having *predestinated us to the adoption of sons,*[3] made us *share the fashion of Christ's glorious body.*[4] Being therefore made *partakers of Christ,*[5] ye are properly called Christs, and of you God said, *Touch not My Christs,*[6] or anointed. Now ye were made Christs,

[1] 1 Cor. 11. 2. [2] Gal. 3. 27. [3] Eph. 1. 5.
[4] Phil. 3. 21. [5] Heb. 3. 14. [6] Ps. 105. 15.

by receiving the emblem of the Holy Ghost; and all things were in a figure wrought in you, because ye are figures of Christ. He also bathed Himself in the river Jordan, and having imparted of the fragrance of His Godhead to the waters, He came up from them; and the Holy Ghost in substance lighted on Him, like resting upon like. In the same manner to you also, after you had come up from the pool of the sacred streams, was given the Unction, the emblem of that wherewith Christ was anointed; and this is the Holy Ghost; of whom also the blessed Esaias, in his prophecy respecting Him, says in the person of the Lord, *The Spirit of the Lord is upon Me, because He hath anointed Me to preach glad tidings to the poor.*[1]

2. For Christ was not anointed by men with oil or material ointment, but the Father having appointed Him to be the Saviour of the whole world, anointed Him with the Holy Ghost, as Peter says, *Jesus of Nazareth, whom God anointed with the Holy Ghost.*[2] And David the Prophet cried, saying, *Thy throne, O God, is for ever and ever; a sceptre of righteousness is the sceptre of Thy kingdom; Thou hast loved righteousness and hated iniquity; therefore God even Thy God hath anointed Thee with the oil of gladness above Thy fellows.*[3] And as Christ was in truth crucified, and buried, and raised, and you in likeness are in Baptism accounted worthy of being crucified, buried, and raised together with Him, so is it with the unction also. As He was anointed with the spiritual oil of gladness, the Holy Ghost, who is so

[1] Is. 61. 1.   [2] Acts 10. 38.   [3] Ps. 45. 6 f.

called, because He is the author of spiritual gladness, so ye were anointed with ointment, having been made partakers and *fellows*[1] of Christ.

3. But beware of supposing this to be plain ointment. For as the Bread of the Eucharist, after the invocation of the Holy Ghost, is mere bread no longer, but the Body of Christ, so also this holy ointment is no more simple ointment, nor (so to say) common, after the invocation, but the gift of Christ; and by the presence of His Godhead, it causes in us the Holy Ghost. It is symbolically applied to thy forehead and thy other senses; and while thy body is anointed with visible ointment, thy soul is sanctified by the Holy and life-giving Spirit.

4. And ye were first anointed on your forehead, that ye might be delivered from the shame, which the first man, when he had transgressed, bore about with him everywhere; and that *with open face ye might behold as in a glass the glory of the Lord*.[2] Then on your ears; that ye might receive ears quick to hear the Divine Mysteries, of which Esaias has said, *The Lord wakened mine ear to hear*;[3] and the Lord Jesus in the Gospel, *He that hath ears to hear let him hear*.[4] Then on your nostrils; that receiving the sacred ointment ye may say, *We are to God a sweet savour of Christ, in them that are saved*.[5] Then on your breast; that having put on the breast-plate of righteousness, ye may stand against the wiles of the devil.[6] For as Christ after His baptism, and the

[1] Ibid. 7.   [2] 2 Cor. 3. 18.   [3] Is. 50. 4.
[4] Mat. 11. 15.   [5] 2 Cor. 2. 15.   [6] Eph. 6. 14 and 11.

descent of the Holy Ghost, went forth and vanquished
the adversary, so likewise, having, after Holy Baptism
and the Mystical Chrism, put on the whole armour of
the Holy Ghost, do ye stand against the power of the
enemy, and vanquish it, saying, *I can do all things
through Christ which strengtheneth me.*[1]

5. When ye are counted worthy of this Holy Chrism,
ye are called Christians, verifying also the name by
your new birth. For before you were vouchsafed this
grace, ye had properly no right to this title, but were
advancing on your way towards being Christians.

6. Moreover, you should know that this Chrism has
its symbol in the old Scripture. For what time Moses
imparted to his brother the command of God, and made
him High-priest, after bathing in water, he anointed
him; and Aaron was called Christ or Anointed, from
the emblematical Chrism. So also the High-priest rais-
ing Solomon to the kingdom, anointed him after he
had bathed in Gihon.[2] To them, however, these things
happened in a figure, but to you not in a figure, but in
truth; because ye were truly anointed by the Holy
Ghost. Christ is the beginning of your salvation; He
is truly the First-fruit, and ye the mass; but if the First-
fruit be holy,[3] it is manifest that Its holiness will pass
to the mass also.

7. Keep This unspotted: for It shall teach you all
things if It abides in you, as you have just heard
declared by the blessed John, who discourses much
concerning this Chrism. For this holy thing is a spiritual

[1] Phil. 4. 13.   [2] 1 Kings 1. 39.   [3] Rom. 11. 16.

preservative of the body, and safeguard of the soul. Of this in ancient times the blessed Esaias prophesying said, *And in this mountain,*—(now he calls the Church a mountain elsewhere also, as when he says, *In the last days the mountain of the Lord's house shall be established ;*)[1] —*in this mountain, shall the Lord make unto all people a feast; they shall drink wine, they shall drink gladness, they shall be anointed with ointment.*[2] And that he may make thee sure, hear what he says of this ointment as being mystical; *Give all these things to the nations, for the counsel of the Lord is unto all nations.*[3] Having been anointed, therefore, with this holy ointment, keep it unspotted and unblemished in you, pressing forward by good works, and becoming well-pleasing to the Captain of your salvation, Christ Jesus, to whom be glory for ever and ever. Amen.

MYSTAGOGICAL CATECHESIS IV

ON THE EUCHARISTIC FOOD

1 Cor. 11. 23

I have received of the Lord that which also I delivered unto you, That the Lord Jesus, the same night in which He was betrayed, took bread, &c.

1. THIS teaching of the Blessed Paul is alone sufficient to give you a full assurance concerning those Divine Mysteries, which when ye are vouchsafed, ye are of *the*

---

[1] Is. 2. 2.   [2] Is. 25. 6. LXX.   [3] Ibid. 7. LXX.

same body[1] and blood with Christ. For he has just distinctly said, *That our Lord Jesus Christ the same night in which He was betrayed, took bread, and when He had given   ιks He brake it, and said, Take, eat, this is My Body: and having taken the cup and given thanks, He said, Take, drink, this is My Blood.*[2] Since then He Himself has declared and said of the Bread, *This is My Body*, who shall dare to doubt any longer? And since He has affirmed and said, *This is My Blood*, who shall ever hesitate, saying, that it is not His blood?

2. He once turned water into wine, in Cana of Galilee, at His own will, and is it incredible that He should have turned wine into blood? That wonderful work He miraculously wrought, when called to an earthly marriage; and shall He not much rather be acknowledged to have bestowed the fruition of His Body and Blood on the children of the bridechamber?

3. Therefore with fullest assurance let us partake as of the Body and Blood of Christ: for in the figure of Bread is given to thee His Body, and in the figure of Wine His Blood; that thou by partaking of the Body and Blood of Christ, mightest be made of the same body and the same blood with Him. For thus we come to bear Christ in us, because His Body and Blood are diffused through our members; thus it is that, according to the blessed Peter, *we become partakers of the divine nature.*[3]

4. Christ on a certain occasion discoursing with the Jews said, *Except ye eat My flesh and drink My blood,*

[1] Eph. 3. 6.   [2] 1 Cor. 11. 23–5.   [3] 2 Pet. 1. 4.

ye have no life in you.[1] They not receiving His saying spiritually were offended, and went backward, supposing that He was inviting them to eat flesh.

5. Even under the Old Testament there was shewbread; but this as it belonged to the Old Testament, came to an end; but in the New Testament there is the Bread of heaven, and the Cup of salvation, sanctifying soul and body; for as the Bread has respect to our body, so is the Word appropriate to our soul.

6. Contemplate therefore the Bread and Wine not as bare elements, for they are, according to the Lord's declaration, the Body and Blood of Christ; for though sense suggests this to thee, let faith stablish thee. Judge not the matter from taste, but from faith be fully assured without misgiving, that thou hast been vouchsafed the Body and Blood of Christ.

7. The blessed David also shall advise thee the meaning of this, saying, *Thou hast prepared a table before me in the presence of mine enemies.*[2] What he says, is to this effect. Before Thy coming, evil spirits prepared a table for men, foul and polluted and full of all devilish influence; but since Thy coming, O Lord, *Thou hast prepared a table before me.* When the man says to God, *Thou hast prepared before me a table*, what other does he mean but that mystical and spiritual Table, which God hath prepared *over against*, that is, contrary and in opposition to the evil spirits? And very truly; for that had fellowship with devils, but this, with God. *Thou has anointed my head with oil.* With oil

[1] John 6. 53.   [2] Ps. 23. 5.

He anointed thine head upon thy forehead, 'by the seal which thou hast of God; that thou mayest be made *the impression of the seal, Holiness of God*.[1] And *my cup runneth over*.[2] Thou seest that cup here spoken of, which Jesus took in His hands, and gave thanks, and said, *This is My blood, which is shed for many for the remission of sins*.[3]

8. Therefore Solomon also, pointing at this grace, says in Ecclesiastes, *Come hither, eat thy bread with joy*, (that is, the spiritual bread; *Come hither*, calling with words of salvation and blessing,) *and drink thy wine with a merry heart;* (that is, the spiritual wine;) *and let thy head lack no ointment*, (thou seest he alludes even to the mystic Chrism;) *and let thy garments be always white, for God now accepteth thy works*[4]; for before thou camest to Baptism, thy works were *vanity of vanities*. But now, having put off thy old garments, and put on those which are spiritually white, thou must be continually robed in white; we mean not this, that thou must always wear white raiment; but with truly white and glistering and spiritual attire, thou must be clothed withal, that thou mayest say with the blessed Esaias, *My soul shall be joyful in my God; for He hath clothed me with the garments of salvation, He hath covered me with the robe of gladness*.[5]

9. These things having learnt, and being fully persuaded that what seems bread is not bread, though bread by taste, but the Body of Christ; and that what

---

[1] Exod. 28. 32. LXX. [2] Ps. 23. 5.   [3] Mat. 26. 28.
[4] Eccles. 9. 7. LXX.   [5] Is. 61. 10. LXX.

seems wine is not wine, though the taste will have it
so, but the Blood of Christ; and that of this David sung
of old, saying, *And bread which strengtheneth man's
heart, and oil to make his face to shine,*[1] 'strengthen
thine heart', partaking thereof as spiritual, and 'make
the face of thy soul to shine'. And so having it un-
veiled by a pure conscience, mayest thou *behold as in
a glass the glory of the Lord*, and proceed from *glory to
glory*,[2] in Christ Jesus our Lord:—To whom be honour,
and might, and glory, for ever and ever. Amen.

MYSTAGOGICAL CATECHESIS V

ON THE EUCHARISTIC RITE

1 Pet. 2. 1

*Wherefore laying aside all malice, and all guile, and
hypocrisies, and envies, and evil speakings, &c.*

1. ON former times of our meeting together ye have
heard sufficiently, by the loving-kindness of God, concerning Baptism, and Chrism, and the partaking of the
Body and Blood of Christ; and now it is necessary to
pass on to what is next in order, meaning today to
give the finish to your spiritual edification.

2. Ye saw then the Deacon give to the Priest water
to wash, and to the Presbyters who stood round God's
altar. He gave it, not at all because of bodily defile-
ment; no; for we did not set out for the Church with

---

[1] Ps. 104. 15.   [2] 2 Cor. 3. 18.

defiled bodies. But this washing of hands is a symbol
that ye ought to be pure from all sinful and unlawful
deeds; for since the hands are a symbol of action, by
washing them we represent the purity and blameless-
ness of our conduct. Hast thou not heard the blessed
David opening this mystery, and saying, *I will wash
my hands in innocency, and so will I compass Thine
Altar, O Lord*?[1] The washing therefore of hands is a
symbol of immunity from sin.

3. Then the Deacon cries aloud, RECEIVE YE ONE
ANOTHER; AND LET US KISS ONE ANOTHER. Think not
that this kiss ranks with those given in public by common friends. It is not such: this kiss blends souls one
with another, and solicits for them entire forgiveness.
Therefore this kiss is the sign that our souls are mingled
together, and have banished all remembrance of wrongs.
For this cause Christ said, *If thou bring thy gift to the
altar, and there rememberest that thy brother hath aught
against thee; leave there thy gift upon the altar, and go thy
way; first be reconciled to thy brother, and then come and
offer thy gift.*[2] The kiss therefore is reconciliation, and
for this reason holy: as the blessed Paul has in his
Epistles urged; *Greet ye one another with a holy kiss*;[3]
and Peter, *with a kiss of charity.*[4]

4. After this the Priest cries aloud, LIFT UP YOUR
HEARTS. For truly ought we in that most awful hour
to have our heart on high with God, and not below,
thinking of earth and earthly things. The Priest then
in effect bids all in that hour abandon all worldly

---

[1] Ps. 26. 6.   [2] Mat. 5. 23.   [3] 1 Cor. 16. 20.   [4] 1 Pet. 5. 14.

thoughts, or household cares, and to have their heart in heaven with the merciful God. Then ye answer, WE LIFT THEM UP UNTO THE LORD: assenting to him, by your avowal. But let no one come here, who with his lips can say 'We lift up our hearts to the Lord', but in mind employs his thoughts on worldly business. God indeed should be in our memory at all times, but if this is impossible by reason of human infirmity, at least in that hour this should be our earnest endeavour.

5. Then the Priest says, LET US GIVE THANKS TO THE LORD. For in good sooth are we bound to give thanks, that He has called us, unworthy as we are, to so great grace; that He has reconciled us who were His foes; that He hath vouchsafed to us the Spirit of adoption. Then ye say, IT IS MEET AND RIGHT: for in giving thanks we do a meet thing and a right; but He did, not a right thing, but what was more than right, when He did us good, and counted us meet for such great benefits.

6. After this we make mention of heaven, and earth, and sea; of the sun and moon; of the stars and all the creation, rational and irrational, visible and invisible; of Angels, Archangels, Virtues, Dominions, Principalities, Powers, Thrones; of the Cherubim with many faces: in effect repeating that call of David's, *Magnify the Lord with me.*[1] We make mention also of the Seraphim, whom Esaias by the Holy Ghost beheld encircling the throne of God, and with two of their wings veiling their countenances, and with two their feet, and with two flying, who cried, HOLY, HOLY,

[1] Ps. 34. 3.

HOLY, LORD GOD OF SABAOTH.[1] For, for this cause rehearse we this confession of God, delivered down to us from the Seraphim, that we may join in Hymns with the hosts of the world above.

7. Then having sanctified ourselves by these spiritual Hymns, we call upon the merciful God to send forth His Holy Spirit upon the gifts lying before Him; that He may make the Bread the Body of Christ, and the Wine the Blood of Christ; for whatsoever the Holy Ghost has touched, is sanctified and changed.

8. Then, after the spiritual sacrifice is perfected, the Bloodless Service upon that Sacrifice of Propitiation, we entreat God for the common peace of the Church, for the tranquillity of the world; for kings; for soldiers and allies; for the sick; for the afflicted; and, in a word, for all who stand in need of succour we all supplicate and offer this Sacrifice.

9. Then we commemorate also those who have fallen asleep before us, first, Patriarchs, Prophets, Apostles, Martyrs, that at their prayers and intervention God would receive our petition. Afterwards also on behalf of the holy Fathers and Bishops who have fallen asleep before us, and in a word of all who in past years have fallen asleep among us, believing that it will be a very great advantage to the souls, for whom the supplication is put up, while that Holy and most Awful Sacrifice is presented.

10. And I wish to persuade you by an illustration. For I know that many say, what is a soul profited,

[1] Cf. Is. 6. 3.

which departs from this world either with sins, or without sins, if it be commemorated in the prayer? Now surely if, when a king had banished certain who had given him offence, their connexions should weave a crown and offer it to him on behalf of those under his vengeance, would he not grant a respite to their punishments? In the same way we, when we offer to Him our supplications for those who have fallen asleep, though they be sinners, weave no crown, but offer up Christ, sacrificed for our sins, propitiating our merciful God both for them and for ourselves.

11. Then, after these things, we say that Prayer which the Saviour delivered to His own disciples, with a pure conscience styling God our Father, and saying, OUR FATHER, WHICH ART IN HEAVEN. O most surpassing loving-kindness of God! On them who revolted from Him and were in the very extreme of misery has He bestowed such complete forgiveness of their evil deeds, and so great participation of grace, as that they should even call Him Father. 'Our Father, which art in heaven'; they also, too, are a heaven who bear the image of the heavenly, in whom God is, *dwelling and walking in them.*[1]

12. HALLOWED BE THY NAME. The Name of God is in its own nature holy, whether we say so or not; but since it is sometimes profaned among sinners, according to the words, *Through you My Name is continually blasphemed among the Gentiles,*[2] we pray that in us God's Name may be hallowed; not that it becomes holy from

---

[1] 2 Cor. 6. 16.   [2] Rom. 2. 24.

not being holy, but because it becomes holy in us, when we become holy, and do things worthy of holiness.

13. THY KINGDOM COME. The clean soul can say with boldness, 'Thy kingdom come'; for he who has heard Paul saying, *Let not sin reign in your mortal body*,[1] but has cleansed himself in deed, thought, and word, will say to God, 'Thy kingdom come'.

14. THY WILL BE DONE AS IN HEAVEN SO IN EARTH. The divine and blessed Angels do the will of God, as David in a Psalm has said, *Bless the Lord, ye His Angels, that excel in strength, that do His commandments*.[2] So then, thou meanest by thy prayer, 'as Thy will is done by the Angels, so be it done on earth also by me, Lord'.

15. GIVE US THIS DAY OUR SUPER-SUBSTANTIAL BREAD. This common bread is not super-substantial bread, but this Holy Bread is super-substantial, that is, appointed for the substance of the soul. For this Bread *goeth* not *into the belly and is cast out into the draught*,[3] but is diffused through all thou art, for the benefit of body and soul. But by *this day*, he means, 'each day', as also Paul has said, *While it is called to-day*.[4]

16. AND FORGIVE US OUR DEBTS AS WE FORGIVE OUR DEBTORS. For we have many sins. For we offend both in word and in thought, and very many things do we worthy of condemnation; and *if we say that we have no sin*,[5] we lie, as John says. And we enter into a

[1] Rom. 6. 12.   [2] Ps. 103. 10.   [3] Mat. 15. 17.
[4] Heb. 3. 13.   [5] 1 John 1. 8.

covenant with God, entreating Him to pardon our sins, as we also forgive our neighbours their debts. Considering then what we receive and for what, let us not put off, nor delay to forgive one another. The offences committed against us are slight and trivial, and easily settled; but those which we have committed against God are great, and call for mercy such as His only is. Take heed, therefore, lest for these small and inconsiderable sins against thyself, thou bar against thyself forgiveness from God for thy most grievous sins.

17. AND LEAD US NOT INTO TEMPTATION, O LORD. Does then the Lord teach to pray thus, viz. that we may not be tempted at all? And how is it said elsewhere, 'the man who is not tempted, is unproved'; and again, *My brethren, count it all joy when ye fall into divers temptations*;[1] or rather does not the entering into temptation mean the being whelmed under the temptation? For the temptation is like a winter-torrent difficult to cross. Some then, being most skilful swimmers, pass over, not being whelmed beneath temptations, nor swept down by them at all; while others who are not such, entering into them sink in them. As for example, Judas entering into the temptation of covetousness, swam not through it, but sinking beneath it was choked both in body and spirit. Peter entered into the temptation of the denial; but having entered it, he was not overwhelmed by it, but manfully swimming through it, he was delivered from the temptation. Listen again, in another place, to the company of

[1] Jam. i. 2.

unscathed saints, giving thanks for deliverance from temptation, *For Thou, O God, hast proved us; Thou hast tried us like as silver is tried. Thou broughtest us into the net; Thou laidest affliction upon our loins. Thou hast caused men to ride over our heads; we went through fire and through water; but thou broughtest us out into a wealthy place.*[1] Thou seest them speaking boldly, because they passed through and were not pierced. *But Thou broughtest us out into a wealthy place;* now their coming into a wealthy place is their being delivered from temptation.

18. BUT DELIVER US FROM THE EVIL. If *Lead us not into temptation* had implied the not being tempted at all, He would not have said, 'But deliver us from the evil'. Now the evil is the Wicked Spirit who is our adversary, from whom we pray to be delivered. Then, after completing the prayer, Thou sayest, AMEN; by this Amen, which means 'So be it', setting thy seal to the petitions of this divinely taught prayer.

19. After this the Priest says, HOLY THINGS TO HOLY MEN. Holy are the gifts presented, since they have been visited by the Holy Ghost; holy are you also, having been vouchsafed the Holy Ghost; the holy things therefore correspond to the holy persons. Then ye say, ONE IS HOLY, ONE IS THE LORD, JESUS CHRIST. For truly One is holy, by nature holy; we, too, are holy, but not by nature, only by participation, and discipline, and prayer.

20. After this ye hear the chanter, with a sacred

_____
[1] Ps. 66. 10–12.

melody inviting you to the communion of the Holy
Mysteries, and saying, *O taste and see that the Lord is
good*.[1] Trust not the decision to thy bodily palate; no,
but to faith unfaltering; for when we taste we are
bidden to taste, not bread and wine, but the sign of
the Body and Blood of Christ.

21. Approaching, therefore, come not with thy wrists
extended, or thy fingers open; but make thy left hand
as if a throne for thy right, which is on the eve of
receiving the King. And having hollowed thy palm,
receive the Body of Christ, saying after it, Amen. Then
after thou hast with carefulness hallowed thine eyes
by the touch of the Holy Body, partake thereof; giving
heed lest thou lose any of it; for what thou losest is
a loss to thee as it were from one of thine own members.
For tell me, if any one gave thee gold dust, wouldest
thou not with all precaution keep it fast, being on thy
guard against losing any of it, and suffering loss? How
much more cautiously then wilt thou observe that not
a crumb falls from thee, of what is more precious than
gold and precious stones?

22. Then after having partaken of the Body of
Christ, approach also to the Cup of His Blood; not
stretching forth thine hands, but bending and saying
in the way of worship and reverence, Amen, be thou
hallowed by partaking also of the Blood of Christ. And
while the moisture is still upon thy lips, touching it
with thine hands, hallow both thine eyes and brow
and the other senses. Then wait for the prayer, and

[1] Ps. 34. 9.

give thanks unto God, who hath accounted thee worthy of so great mysteries.

23. Hold fast these traditions unspotted, and keep yourselves free from offence. Sever not yourselves from the Communion; deprive not yourselves, by the pollution of sins, of these Holy and Spiritual Mysteries. *And the God of peace sanctify you wholly; and may your whole spirit, and soul, and body be preserved blameless unto the coming of our Lord Jesus Christ:*[1]—To whom be glory and honour and might, with the Father and the Holy Spirit, now and ever, and world without end. Amen.

[1] 1 Thess. 5. 23.

INDEX OF PROPER NAMES